PRACTICE MAKES PERFECT

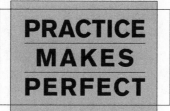

Advanced English Grammar

for ESL Learners

PRACTICE
MAKES
PERFECT

Advanced English Grammar
for ESL Learners

Mark Lester

McGraw Hill

New York Chicago San Francisco Lisbon London Madrid Mexico City
Milan New Delhi San Juan Seoul Singapore Sydney Toronto

Contents

Preface

Practice Makes Perfect: Advanced English Grammar for ESL Learners is designed to help advanced-level learners gain control over difficult areas of English grammar. This book is not a systematic treatment of all areas of English grammar. Instead, it deals in depth with selected grammar topics that pose special problems for nonnative speakers. These topics fall into two areas: (1) areas of grammar that are the source of persistent error and (2) areas of grammar that are so complex that even advanced nonnative speakers almost always avoid them.

Examples of the first type of persistent error would be using wrong articles, misusing the present and present progressive tenses, confusing present and past participles of verbs used as adjectives, and using the wrong relative pronoun in adjective clauses.

Examples of the second type of constructions that are avoided because of their complexity would be gerunds and infinitives used as nouns, participial phrases, and *wh-* infinitive phrases.

Each topic is explained in detail, often going far beyond what would be found in a more general grammar book. My hope is that by fully understanding the technical grammatical issues involved, you will feel much more confident in using these difficult constructions. Each bit of grammatical analysis is supported by a series of practice exercises that will help you gain practical control over the issues covered in the analysis.

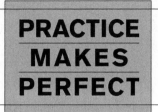

**PRACTICE
MAKES
PERFECT**

Advanced English Grammar
for ESL Learners

Noun plurals

This chapter deals with three topics: (1) the spelling and pronunciation of the regular plural, (2) irregular plurals of English and Latin origin, and (3) noncount nouns, an important group of nouns that are always singular in form but not in meaning.

The spelling and pronunciations of regular nouns

Spelling

Most regular nouns form their plural spelling by adding -s to the singular form. For example:

SINGULAR	PLURAL
boat	boats
plane	planes
ski	skis

If the regular plural is pronounced as a separate syllable rhyming with *fizz*, the regular plural is spelled -es. For example:

SINGULAR	PLURAL
batch	batches
box	boxes
bus	buses
wish	wishes

There is a special spelling rule for the plural of words that end in a consonant + *y*: change the *y* to *i* and add -es. For example:

SINGULAR	PLURAL
baby	babies
family	families
lady	ladies
story	stories

However, if the *y* follows a vowel, the *y* is part of the spelling of the vowel and cannot be changed. For example:

SINGULAR	PLURAL
day	days
key	keys
toy	toys

EXERCISE
1·1

Write the correct form of the plural in the second column. The first question is done as an example.

flash   *flashes*

SINGULAR   PLURAL

1. delay _____
2. tool _____
3. stone _____
4. fly _____
5. neck _____
6. switch _____
7. library _____
8. path _____
9. guess _____
10. valley _____

Pronunciation

The regular plural has three different pronunciations: /s/, /z/, and /əz/ (rhymes with *fizz*). Which one we use is totally governed by the sound that immediately precedes it according to the following three rules:

1. If the singular noun ends in a voiceless consonant sound (except a voiceless sibilant sound like the *s* in *bus* or *sh* in *wish*), then the plural is formed with the voiceless sibilant /s/. The voiceless consonants are spelled *p* (*stop*); *t* (*hat*); *c* (*comic*); *ck* (*clock*); *k* (*lake*); *f* (*cliff*); *gh* (if pronounced as an /f/ sound as in *cough*); and *th* (if voiceless like *path*).

2. If the singular noun ends in a vowel sound or a voiced consonant sound (except a voiced sibilant sound like in *fuzz*), then the plural is formed with the voiced sibilant /z/. The voiced consonants are spelled *b* (*tube*); *d* (*road*); *g* (*fog*), *dge* (*hedge*); *ve* (*wave*), *l* (*bell*); *m* (*home*); *n* (*tune*); and *ng* (*ring*).

3. If the singular noun ends in a consonant with a sibilant sound, either voiceless or voiced, then the plural is pronounced as a separate unstressed syllable /əz/ rhyming with *buzz*. The most common sibilant consonants are spelled *ce* (*face*); *s* (*bus*); *sh* (*dish*); *tch* (*watch*); *ge* (*page*); *z* (*blaze*); *se* (*nose*).

EXERCISE

1·2

Write the correct form of the plural in the correct column. (Hint: Say the words out loud. If you whisper or say them to yourself, voiced sounds will be automatically de-voiced so they will sound the same as voiceless sounds.) The first question is done as an example.

SINGULAR FORM	/S/	/Z/	/əZ/
face			*faces*
1. clock			
2. hedge			
3. colleague			
4. phone			
5. allowance			
6. song			

7. river   _____   _____   _____

8. moth   _____   _____   _____

9. tree   _____   _____   _____

10. mist   _____   _____   _____

11. garage   _____   _____   _____

12. box   _____   _____   _____

13. love   _____   _____   _____

14. trick   _____   _____   _____

15. zoo   _____   _____   _____

Irregular plurals of English and Latin origin

English origin

Not surprisingly, most irregular plurals are of English origin. Three different types of plurals retain archaic patterns of forming plurals that were common in older forms of English. Seven nouns form their plurals by a vowel change alone:

SINGULAR	PLURAL
foot	feet (see note)
goose	geese
louse	lice
man	men
mouse	mice
tooth	teeth
woman	women

Note: In addition to the usual plural form *feet*, the noun *foot* has a second plural form *foot*. We use this plural to refer to length or measurements. For example:

We need a ten-**foot** ladder.
Harry is now six **foot** four inches tall.

A small number of nouns that refer to fish and animals retain an old zero-form plural that makes plural nouns look just like singular nouns. For example:

SINGULAR	PLURAL
one cod	two cod
one fish	two fish
one sheep	two sheep
one shrimp	two shrimp

Since the singular and plural forms of these nouns are identical, the actual number of the noun can only be determined by subject-verb agreement or by the use of articles. For example:

Singular	The sheep **was** caught in the fence.
Plural	The sheep **were** caught in the fence.
Singular	**A** sheep stood in the middle of the road.
Plural	**Some** sheep stood in the middle of the road.

Three nouns retain the plural ending *-en* that in Old English was standard for regular nouns:

SINGULAR	PLURAL
ox	oxen
child	children
brother	brethren (see note)

Note: *Brethren* is used only for members of a religious order or congregation of men. The more commonly used plural is *brothers*.

Finally there is a fourth group of irregular plurals that reflects a phonological rule in Old English. In Old English, the letter *f* had two completely predictable pronunciations: /f/ at the beginning and ends of words, and /v/ in the middle of words. We can still see today this alternation between /f/ and /v/ in the singular and plural of most native English words that end in *-f*: the *f* changes to *v* (reflecting the pronunciation) when we add the *-es* plural ending and put the *f* in the middle of the word. For example:

SINGULAR	PLURAL
half	halves
life	lives
thief	thieves

Write the correct form of the plural in the second column. The first question is done as an example.

deer   *deer*

SINGULAR   PLURAL

1. tooth _____
2. loaf _____
3. goose _____
4. shelf _____
5. ox _____
6. trout _____
7. knife _____
8. mouse _____
9. wolf _____
10. cliff _____

Latin plurals

Beginning in the Renaissance, English adopted thousands of words directly from classical Latin. Often the original Latin forms of the plural were also borrowed. While the irregularity of Latin grammar is astonishing, there are two patterns of forming the plural of Latin nouns that are common enough to be well worth knowing:

◆ **Plurals of Latin nouns ending in -*us*.** The plurals of these nouns typically end in -*i*. For example:

SINGULAR	PLURAL
alumnus	alumni
focus	foci
locus	loci

◆ **Plurals of Latin nouns that end in -*um*.** The plurals of these nouns typically end in -*a*. For example:

SINGULAR	PLURAL
addendum	addenda
curriculum	curricula
datum	data (see note)

Note: The Latin plural *data* is used in formal academic and scientific writing. For example:

The **data** are very clear.

However, in conversation and informal writing, we often use *data* as a kind of collective singular. For example:

The **data** is very clear.

Write the correct form of the plural in the second column. The first question is done as an example.

stratum   *strata*
_____

SINGULAR   PLURAL

1. stimulus   _____

2. memorandum   _____

3. syllabus   _____

4. spectrum   _____

5. consortium   _____

Noncount nouns

Noncount nouns are names for categories of things. For example, the noncount noun *housing* is a collective term that refers to an entire category of places where people temporarily or permanently reside, such as *room, house, apartment, flat, dormitory, condo, tent,* and so on. The distinctive grammatical feature of noncount nouns is that they cannot be counted with number words or used in the plural, as opposed to **count** nouns, which can be used with number words and be used in the plural. For example:

Noncount	X one housing, X two housings.
Count	one room, two rooms
	one house, two houses
	one apartment, two apartments
	one flat, two flats
	one dormitory, two dormitories
	one condo, two condos
	one tent, two tents

Note: the symbol X is used throughout the book to indicate that the following word, phrase, or sentence is ungrammatical.

An especially important feature of noncount nouns is that they cannot be used with the indefinite article *a/an* because *a/an* are historically forms of the number *one*. So, for example we can say *a room, a house, an apartment*, and so forth, but we cannot say X *a housing*.

English has a large number of noncount nouns. Most noncount nouns fall into one of the ten semantic categories listed below:

CATEGORY	EXAMPLES
Abstractions	beauty, faith, luck
Academic fields	chemistry, economics, physics (see note)

Note: Despite the final *-s, economics* and *physics* are singular.

Food	butter, meat, salt
Gerunds (*-ing* verb forms used as nouns)	running, smiling, winning
Languages	Arabic, English, Spanish
Liquids and gases	air, blood, gasoline
Materials	cement, paper, wood
Natural phenomena	electricity, matter, space
Sports and games	baseball, chess, soccer
Weather words	fog, rain, wind

The following words are all noncount nouns. Put each noun into the category that is most appropriate for it. The first word is done as an example.

beer, charity, cheese, Chinese, coffee, football, geology, glass, gold, gravity, hope, knowledge, laughing, literature, oxygen, pepper, poker, rice, Russian, sleeping, snow, sunshine, talking, time, wool

Category

Abstractions: _____

Academic fields: _____

Food: _____

Gerunds: _____

Languages: _____

Liquids and gases: *beer* _____

Materials: _____

Natural phenomena: _____

Sports and games: _____

Weather words: _____

Possessive nouns and personal pronouns

·2·

This chapter deals with three topics: (1) the correct forms of possessive nouns and personal pronouns, (2) the different meanings of possessive nouns and personal pronouns, and (3) possessives formed with *of*.

The correct forms of possessive nouns and personal pronouns

Possessive nouns and pronouns have the same functions but are formed in very different ways.

The possessive form of nouns

Up until the sixteenth century the plural -*s* and the possessive -*s* were spelled exactly the same way: -*s*. Beginning in the sixteenth century, people began distinguishing the two different grammatical endings by marking the possessive -*s* with an apostrophe. For example:

Plural -s	boys	girls	friends	schools
Possessive -s:	boy's	girl's	friend's	school's

Note: The origin of this use of the apostrophe is odd. In the late middle ages, people (mistakenly) thought that the possessive -*s* was a contraction of *his*. For example, *John's book* was thought to be a contraction of *John, his book*. Thus the apostrophe was introduced to indicate the missing letters of *his* in the same way that the apostrophe in *doesn't* indicates the missing *o* in the contraction of *not*. Despite the nonsensical rationale for this use of the apostrophe, the idea of using the apostrophe to distinguish between the two *meanings* had become firmly established by Shakespeare's time. The use of the apostrophe *after* the -*s* to signal the possessive use of the plural noun did not become universally accepted until the nineteenth century.

We now have this apparent three-way distinction among the three *forms*: plural -*s*, singular possessive -'*s*, and plural possessive -*s*':

Plural	boys	girls	friends	schools
Singular possessive	boy's	girl's	friend's	school's
Plural possessive	boys'	girls'	friends'	schools'

While it is correct to call -*s*' the plural possessive, it is a mistake is to think of the -'*s* as the singular possessive. The problem with this definition arises with the possessive forms of irregular nouns that become plural without adding a plural -*s*, for example:

SINGULAR		PLURAL	
NOUN	POSSESSIVE	NOUN	POSSESSIVE
man	man's	men	**men's**
woman	woman's	women	**women's**
datum	datum's	data	**data's**
sheep	sheep's	sheep	**sheep's**

As you can see, -'*s* is used with these plural possessive nouns, not -*s*'. This is not some kind of strange exception to the general rule about plurals and possessives. It actually makes perfect sense: if we used -*s*' with these irregular nouns, it would mean (incorrectly, of course) that this -*s* is what makes these nouns plural. Actually, the -*s* has nothing to do with these nouns being plural; the only function of this -*s* is to show possession.

A much better way to think of the plural and possessive -*s*' is the following:

PLURAL ONLY	POSSESSIVE ONLY	BOTH PLURAL AND POSSESSIVE
-s	-'s	-s'

Usually -'*s* is attached to singular nouns. However, in the case of irregular nouns, -'*s* is attached to the plural form to show that the plural form is possessive. In other words, -'*s* means that whatever kind of noun the -'*s* is attached to (singular regular noun or plural irregular noun), that noun is now marked as being possessive. The -*s*' is really the special case in which the -*s* is playing two different and unrelated roles at the same time: (1) making the noun plural and (2) making the noun possessive. This analysis will ensure that you will always use the right form for both regular and irregular nouns.

Fill in the correct forms of the plural and possessives. An example is provided.

	SINGULAR		PLURAL	
NOUN	POSSESSIVE	NOUN		POSSESSIVE
teacher	*teacher's*	*teachers*		*teachers'*
1. mouse				
2. thief				
3. child				
4. goose				
5. ox				
6. deer				
7. foot				
8. tooth				
9. fish				
10. wolf				

The possessive form of personal pronouns

Like other personal pronouns, the possessive pronoun has two numbers (singular and plural) and three persons: first person (speaker); second person (person spoken to); and third person (person or thing spoken about). Possessive personal pronouns differ from possessive nouns in that there are two distinct forms for each possessive pronoun. One form functions as an adjective; that is, the pronoun modifies a following noun. The other form functions as a true pronoun; that is, the pronoun stands by itself in place of a noun. Here is an example using the first person singular pronoun:

Adjective function	That is **my** coat.
Pronoun function	That coat is **mine**.

The two forms are not interchangeable:

> X This is **mine** coat.
> X That coat is **my**.

There is no standard terminology for the two different pronoun functions. In this book we will refer to possessive pronouns that function as adjectives as **adjectival possessive pronouns**. We will refer to possessive pronouns that function as true pronouns as **pronominal possessive pronouns**. Here is a complete list of both types of possessive pronouns:

VOCABULARY

Possessive pronouns

	ADJECTIVAL FORM	PRONOMINAL FORM
Singular		
First person	my	mine
Second person	your	yours
Third person	his	his
	her	hers
	its	its
Plural		
First person	our	ours
Second person	your	yours
Third person	their	theirs

There are several common mistakes with apostrophes when we use the possessive pronominal forms that end in *-s* (*yours, hers, its, ours, yours*, and *theirs*). We so strongly associate apostrophes with possessive noun forms that end in *-s* that it is easy to mistakenly extend the apostrophe to possessive pronouns that also end in *-s*. For example:

> I found John's books. X Did you find **your's**?
> Our friends' reservation is for Tuesday. X When is **their's** for?

Distinguishing between *its* and *it's*

One of the most common errors in written English is confusing the third person singular pronoun *its* with *it's*, the contracted form of *it is*. The major causes of the confusion is that the apostrophe in *it's* is associated with the meaning of possession so that as a result we incorrectly use *it's* as the possessive. For example:

> X My car lost **it's** windshield wiper.
> X The dog already got **it's** treat.

The simplest and most reliable way to distinguish the contracted form of *it is* from the uncontracted possessive pronoun *its* is to see if you can expand *its* or *it's* to *it is*. If the expanded two-word expression makes sense, then you know that you should use the contracted form *it's*. If the expanded two-word expression makes no sense at all, then you know that you are dealing with the possessive pronoun and that you should NOT use the apostrophe.

Here is this test applied to the two example sentences above:

> X My car lost **it's** windshield wiper.
> *Expanded*   X My car lost **it is** windshield wiper.

The expanded form *it is windshield wiper* makes no sense, so we know that *it's* is actually a possessive pronoun that should be spelled without the apostrophe:

> My car lost **its** windshield wiper.

Here is the same technique applied to the second example:

> X The dog already got **it's** treat.
> *Expanded*   X The dog already got **it is** treat.

The expanded form *it is treat* makes no sense, so again we know that *it's* is really an uncontracted possessive pronoun:

> The dog already got **its** treat.

Expand the its *and* it's *in the following sentences and then write the corrected form under the expanded form. If the original is already correct, write "OK" under the expanded form. The first two questions are done as examples.*

Our team lost it's best player.

Expanded   *it is*

Correction   *its*

It's a beautiful day for an outing.

Expanded   *It is*

Correction   *OK*

1. The train just came in. Its on Track 7.

Expanded _____

Correction _____

2. The kitchen needs its windows cleaned.

Expanded _____

Correction _____

3. The store is cutting back on it's hours.

Expanded _____

Correction _____

4. I think its a big mistake to do it.

Expanded _____

Correction _____

5. The drug will lose it's effectiveness with extensive use.

Expanded _____

Correction _____

6. Its a good investment.

Expanded _____

Correction _____

7. The government expressed its opposition to the treaty.

Expanded _____

Correction _____

8. The city had totally redesigned it's website.

Expanded _____

Correction _____

9. The balloon was slowly losing its air.

Expanded _____

Correction _____

10. Its not easy to cash a check from a foreign bank.

Expanded _____

Correction _____

The different meanings of possessive nouns and personal pronouns

There are a number of different meanings in the way possessive nouns and personal pronouns are used. Listed below are the five most common.

1. **Possession.** The single most common use of possessive nouns and pronouns—to show ownership or possession. For example:

   The family's car / **their** car

2. **Association.** People or things associated with the possessive noun or pronoun. For example:

> **Ralph's** neighborhood / **his** neighborhood
> **Susan's** doctor / **her** doctor

Note: Ralph does not own his neighborhood nor does Susan own her doctor.

3. **Attribute.** A characteristic, part, or feature of the possessive noun or pronoun. For example:

> **Emily's** red hair / **her** red hair
> **Jack's** quick temper / **his** quick temper

4. **Action.** Some mental or physical action performed by the noun or pronoun. For example:

> **The editor's** decision / **her** decision
> **The company's** determination to succeed / **its** determination to succeed

5. **Measurement.** An expression of value or time. For example:

> **The dollar's** declining worth / **its** declining worth
> **An hour's** delay / **its** delay

EXERCISE
2·3

In the blank space after each sentence, write the meaning of the underlined phrase. Use one of the following five categories: (1) possession, (2) association, (3) attribute, (4) action, (5) measurement. The first question is done as an example.

Alice's determination grew even stronger. (3) _____*attribute*_____

1. The lawyer asked for <u>a week's postponement</u> of the trial. _____

2. <u>Joan's friends</u> discouraged her from seeing him again. _____

3. <u>John's interference</u> with another player resulted in a penalty. _____

4. This morning, I took <u>Sally's lunch</u> by mistake. _____

5. <u>The court's refusal</u> to hear the case came as a shock. _____

6. <u>Jason's cheerful nature</u> made everyone like him. _____

7. We sent out invitations to <u>the couples' friends and relatives.</u> _____

8. They decided to take <u>a week's vacation</u> in Colorado. _____

9. <u>The judge's decisions</u> are final. _____

10. <u>Everyone's investments</u> had declined about 40 percent. _____

Possessive formed with *of*

In addition to the kinds of possessives we have examined so far (which we will now call **s possessives**), English can also show possession by the use of the preposition *of*. We will call possessives formed this way ***of* possessives**. Here are some examples where both types of possessives can be used:

S POSSESSIVE	OF POSSESSIVE
today's newspaper headlines	the newspaper headlines of today
the city's population	the population of the city
Shakespeare's plays	the plays of Shakespeare
The court's decision	the decision of the court

While the *s* and *of* possessives mean the same thing and are usually interchangeable, there are a number of cases in which they are not interchangeable. To a large extent, the meaning of the possessive determines whether the two forms of the possessive are interchangeable or not. Let us look at the five different meanings of the possessive we discussed above and see how compatible they are with the *of* possessive:

Possession

Here are some examples of possession with both types of possessives.

S POSSESSIVE	OF POSSESSIVE
the family's car	X the car of the family
the dog's bone	X the bone of the dog
the company's trucks	X the trucks of the company

Clearly, the *s* possessive is strongly preferred in the meaning of possession.

Associations

Here are some examples of associations with both types of possessives.

S POSSESSIVE	OF POSSESSIVE
Ralph's neighborhood	X the neighborhood of Ralph
Susan's doctor	X the doctor of Susan
the building's neighborhood	The neighborhood of the building

With this group, there is distinction between animate and inanimate possessive nouns. When the possessive noun is inanimate, both *s* and *of* possessives are used.

Attributes

Here are some examples of attributes with both types of possessives.

S POSSESSIVE	OF POSSESSIVE
Emily's red hair	X the red hair of Emily
Jack's quick temper	X the quick temper of Jack
the building's entryway	the entryway of the building

With this group also, there is distinction between animate and inanimate possessive nouns. When the possessive noun is inanimate, both *s* and *of* possessives are permitted.

Action

Here are some examples of action with both types of possessives.

S POSSESSIVE	OF POSSESSIVE
the editor's decision	the decision of the editor
the company's determination	the determination of the company
the government's reaction	the reaction of the government

This group permits both *s* and *of* possessives equally.

Measurement

Here are some examples of measurement with both types of possessives.

S POSSESSIVE	OF POSSESSIVE
the dollar's declining worth	the declining worth of the dollar
an hour's delay	the delay of an hour
the stock's value	the value of the stock
a second's hesitation	the hesitation of a second

This group also permits both *s* and *of* possessive equally.

EXERCISE 2·4

Below are s possessive phrases. In the space provided, write the of possessive form if it is grammatical. If it is not, write "ungrammatical." The first two questions are done as examples.

the game's rules   *the rules of the game*

my parents' bank   *ungrammatical*

1. two years' duration _____

2. William's backyard _____

3. the lawyer's recommendation _____

4. the yen's status _____

5. the airport's runway _____

6. Mary's knee _____

7. Roberta's boss _____

8. my aunt's best dishes _____

9. the tissue's firmness _____

10. Mr. Brown's proposal _____

Articles and quantifiers

This chapter focuses on two types of noun modifiers that are very trouble-some for nonnative speakers: (1) articles and (2) quantifiers.

Articles and quantifiers are types of **determiners,** a collective term for all noun modifiers that precede adjectives. There are four types of determiners: **articles, possessives, demonstratives,** and **quantifiers**:

Article	**the** book
Possessive	**my** book
Demonstrative	**this** book
Quantifier	**many** books

This chapter focuses on the two types of determiners that are most likely to cause you problems: (1) **articles** and (2) **quantifiers.** Here is an example of each type:

Article	I got **a** good seat for the flight.
	article adj noun
Quantifier	We don't have **many** good options left.
	quantifier adj noun

Articles and quantifiers are different from adjectives and other determiners in that the choice of article and quantifier is determined in part by whether the noun being modified is **count** or **noncount**. (Neither possessives nor demonstratives are affected by this distinction.)

Most common nouns are count nouns, that is, they can be used with number words like *one, two, three,* and the nouns can be used in either the singular or the plural. For example the nouns *book* and *woman* are count nouns:

> one book, two books, three books
> one woman, two women, three women

Note that even nouns like *deer* and *fish* that have no distinct plural forms are still count nouns:

> one deer, two deer, three deer
> one fish, two fish, three fish

We can also see that irregular nouns like *deer* and *fish* have both singular and plural uses by whether the singular or plural verb form is used. For example, using the noun *deer* as a subject, we can see the verb *be* changes form, from singular to plural, in agreement with the number of the subject:

Singular	The deer **is** in the garden again.
Plural	The deer **are** in the garden again.

English has a large number of noncount nouns. These nouns cannot be used with number words. Here are some examples with the noncount nouns *luck, air,* and *butter*:

X one luck, two lucks, three lucks
X one air, two airs, three airs
X one butter, two butters, three butters

Noncount nouns are always used in agreement with singular verb forms, for example:

Luck **has** not been good to me lately.
Warm air **carries** more moisture than dry air.
Butter **is** probably better for you than margarine.

The fact that these nouns agree with singular verbs does not mean that the nouns are singular in meaning. They are neither singular nor plural in meaning; they stand outside the concept of number altogether.

Chapter 1, "Noun plurals," contains a detailed discussion of noncount nouns. Repeated below for your convenience is the key chart that lists the most common types of noncount nouns.

Most noncount nouns fall into one of the ten semantic categories listed below:

CATEGORY	EXAMPLES
Abstractions	beauty, faith, luck
Academic fields	chemistry, economics, physics (See note)

Note: Despite the final -*s*, *economics* and *physics* are singular.

Food	butter, meat, salt
Gerunds (-*ing* verb forms used as nouns)	running, smiling, winning
Languages	Arabic, English, Spanish
Liquids and gases	air, blood, gasoline
Materials	cement, paper, wood
Natural phenomena	electricity, matter, space
Sports and games	baseball, chess, soccer
Weather words	fog, rain, wind

Articles

There are two types of articles: **definite** and **indefinite**.

Using the definite article

The definite article is *the*. The definite article can be used with all types of common nouns: singular, plural, and noncount. For example:

Singular nouns	The **book** is on the desk.
	The **woman** was obviously new to the area.
Plural nouns	The **books** are on the desk.
	The **women** were obviously new to the area.
Noncount nouns	He has all the **luck**.
	The **air** was getting hotter by the minute.
	The **butter** is always kept in the refrigerator.

The definite article is easy to use since it does not change form. The hard part is knowing WHEN to use it.

Use the definite article only if BOTH of the following conditions are met:

- You have a specific person, place, thing, or idea in mind, and
- You can reasonably assume that the reader or listener will know which specific person, place, thing, or idea you mean.

The second of these two conditions is usually met in one of the following four ways:

1. **Previous mention.** Use the definite article with a noun if you have already introduced the noun to the reader or listener. For example:

    I just heard about Tom's accident. Do you know when **the** accident happened?

    We use the definite article with the noun *accident* in the second sentence because the noun had already been introduced in the first sentence.

2. **Defined by modifiers.** Use the definite article with a noun if that noun is followed by modifiers that serve to uniquely define the noun. For example:

    The printer that I bought on sale last week turned out to be defective.

    Even if the printer has not been mentioned previously, the adjective clause *that I bought on sale last week* tells the reader or listener which printer is being talked about.

3. **Uniqueness.** Use the definite article with nouns that refer to things that are one of a kind. For example:

> **The** sun had already set by the time we got home.

There is only one sun, so it is defined by its own uniqueness.

4. **Normal expectations.** Use the definite article with a noun if that noun is something that we would reasonably expect to find or to occur in the context of the sentence. Here are some examples:

> I opened the book and looked at **the** table of contents.

We expect books to have tables of contents.

> **The** laces on my shoes came untied.

We expect shoes to have laces.

> I went into my office and turned on **the** computer.

We expect offices to have computers.

EXERCISE
3·1

State which of the four reasons for using the definite article applies to the definite articles in bold: (1) previous mention, (2) defined by modifiers, (3) uniqueness, or (4) normal expectations. The first question is done as an example.

We were driving in **the** left lane when we had a flat tire. (4) _normal expectaions_

1. We need to deposit all **the** checks that we received yesterday. _____

2. Storms were forming along **the** equator. _____

3. I never found **the** necklace I bought in Greece. _____

4. You should replace **the** windshield wiper in your car. _____

5. Olympia is **the** capital of Washington state. _____

6. I just got **the** memo that you sent this morning. _____

7. Are you connected to **the** Internet? _____

8. They just bought a new boat. They hope to use **the** boat this summer. _____

9. A waiter I hadn't seen before handed out **the** menus. _____

10. **The** verbs in most languages distinguish between present and past time. _____

11. His performance was disappointing. I thought **the** performance lacked conviction. _____

12. Take **the** bus that goes down Elm Street. _____

13. Our kids love to go to Sunset Beach and play in **the** sand. _____

14. There is a package here for Ms. Brown. Take **the** package to her office. _____

15. I need to have a doctor look at **the** mole on my left hand. _____

Using indefinite articles

There are two indefinite articles: *a/an* (used with singular count nouns) and *some* (used with plural count nouns and all noncount nouns). Here are some examples:

Singular count nouns

I have **a** problem.
There is **a** truck parked in front of our house.
I thought of **an** answer to the question.

Plural count nouns

I have **some** problems with that.
There are **some** trucks parked in front of our house.
I thought of **some** answers to the question.

Noncount nouns

Would you like **some** coffee?
There is **some** confusion about the time of the meeting.
People need to have **some** protein every day.

We use indefinite articles in two situations:

1. When we are speaking hypothetically or in general terms and do not have a specific noun in mind, or more commonly

2. When we have a specific noun in mind but know that the listener or reader cannot possibly know which noun it is.

Here is an example of the first situation:

When you fly these days, you have to expect **some** delays.

In this example, the speaker does not have any specific delay in mind because the speaker is talking hypothetically about all airplane travel.

More often, however, we use indefinite articles to signal to readers or listeners that we do not expect them to know which noun we are talking about. Here are some examples:

> I would like you to meet **a** friend of mine. (singular count noun)
> I would like you to meet **some** friends of mine. (plural count noun)
> I need to get **some** information from you. (noncount noun)

The speaker of these sentences uses the indefinite articles because the speaker knows that the audience cannot possibly know which friend or friends the speaker has in mind.

EXERCISE
3·2

Fill in the blank with the appropriate indefinite article: a/an or some. The first question is done as an example. Remember, a is used before consonant sounds and an is used before vowel sounds.

He made me _____*an*_____ offer that I couldn't refuse.

1. The forecast is for _____ rain tonight.

2. There was _____ note on my desk.

3. I noticed that _____ page was missing from the report.

4. I noticed that _____ pages were missing from the report.

5. In _____ circumstances, it would be OK.

6. You need to make _____ reservation as soon as possible.

7. The lawyer gave her _____ advice about drafting her will.

8. It is only _____ suggestion.

9. There was _____ disappointment at the inconclusive outcome.

10. We have finally made _____ progress in resolving the dispute.

Some is used without restriction with both plural nouns and noncount nouns in positive statements:

Plural nouns

We had to get **some** new maps for the trip.
There are **some** apples in the refrigerator.

Noncount nouns

The committee had **some** disagreement about the final wording.
There is **some** fruit in the refrigerator.

However, in negative statements, *any* is used in place of *some*:

Plural nouns

We didn't have to get **any** new maps for the trip.
There aren't **any** apples in the refrigerator.

Noncount nouns

The committee didn't have **any** disagreement about the final wording.
There isn't **any** fruit in the refrigerator.

The use of *some* in negative statements is ungrammatical:

X We didn't have to get **some** new maps for the trip.
X There aren't **some** apples in the refrigerator.
X The committee didn't have **some** disagreement about the final wording.
X There isn't **some** fruit in the refrigerator.

EXERCISE
3·3

Use some *or* any *as appropriate in the following positive and negative statements. The first question is done as an example.*

There aren't _____ *any* _____ meetings scheduled for Friday afternoon.

1. _____ reporters are beginning to ask questions.

2. He certainly didn't show _____ concern about the outcome.

3. _____ rice always sticks to the bottom of the cooking pot.

4. The store didn't have _____ brown rice.

5. There are _____ big mountains to the west of here.

6. I certainly didn't receive _____ encouragement to go ahead.

7. _____ responses were quite favorable.

8. I didn't like _____ choices that were open to us.

9. We need to get _____ gas before we leave town.

10. We won't be able to get _____ gas before we reach Albuquerque.

Some and *any* can both be used in questions, but with different implications. *Some* has the implication that there will be a positive response to the question. *Some* is also used as a polite invitation to do something. *Any* is much more neutral; the speaker is not necessarily anticipating a positive response. Here are two examples that illustrate the difference:

> Would you like **some** coffee? (Waiter asking a customer in a restaurant)
> Do you have **any** maps of France? (Customer asking a clerk in a bookstore)

In the first question, the waiter uses *some* in part because the waiter can reasonably assume that the answer to the question will be positive and in part as a polite encouragement for the customer to have more coffee.

In the second question, the customer uses *any* rather than *some* to signal that he genuinely does not know if the store carries maps of France or not. In other words, the customer does not necessarily expect a positive answer. Now suppose the customer in the bookstore asked the question this way:

> Could I see **some** maps of France?

In this question, the customer is expressing an expectation that the store does actually have maps of France and that the answer will be positive.

The same set of expectations holds for negative questions. *Some* tends to anticipate a positive response, while *any* is more neutral. To see the difference, compare the following two negative questions asked of a child by a parent:

> Don't you have **some** homework?
> Don't you have **any** homework?

The use of *some* in the first question assumes a positive response (so much so that this is virtually a rhetorical question). The use of *any* in the second question implies that the parent genuinely does not know whether or not the child has homework to do.

Use some or any *as appropriate to whether the speaker's expectation is positive or neutral. The first question is done as an example.*

(neutral) Do you think _____*any*_____ flights have been canceled?

1. (positive) Aren't there _____ clean shirts in the closet?

2. (neutral) Did he show _____ remorse for what he had done?

3. (neutral) Did you form _____ impression of the judge's response?

4. (positive) Could they have made _____ errors in recording the data?

5. (neutral) Do you have _____ idea about what happened?

6. (neutral) Were _____ passengers injured in the accident?

7. (positive) Aren't _____ games more important than others?

8. (neutral) Have _____ ballots been challenged by the observers?

9. (neutral) Do _____ passenger trains stop at that station anymore?

10. (positive) Don't _____ professors still grade on a curve?

Turn the first five sentences into questions and the second five sentences into negative statements. In both questions and negative statements, assume a positive expectation using any. *The first question is done as an example.*

Questions

There was some criticism of the proposal.

> *Was there any criticism of the proposal?*

1. They came to some agreement about the contract.

_____

2. Some cars got stuck in the snow.

_____

3. There are some direct flights left.

_____

4. He ordered some soup.

_____

5. There was some frost during the night.

_____

Negative statements

6. She had some congestion this morning.

_____

7. They will take some time off.

_____

8. There are some apartments available.

_____

9. I saw some empty boxes at the grocery store.

_____

10. I have had some pain in my wrist.

_____

Making categorical statements without any articles

Common nouns are so often modified by articles or other determiners that we might conclude that articles or other determiners are obligatory with common nouns. They are with one major exception: when we want to talk about something as a whole category rather than as an individual member of that category. We do this by using noncount nouns or plural count nouns without articles or any other kind of determiners.

Compare the following sentences that use the same noncount noun *wood*:

> The **wood** on the deck needs refinishing.
> We are going to need some **wood**.
> **Wood** is usually more expensive than plastic.

In the first sentence, the use of the definite article *the* signals that the audience of this sentence knows which wood the speaker is talking about—the wood on a particular deck.

In the second sentence, the use of the indefinite article *some* signals that the topic of wood is being introduced for the first time and that the audience of the sentence isn't expected to already know which specific wood the speaker has in mind.

In the third sentence, the absence of any article modifying the noun *wood* means that the speaker is talking in general terms about wood as a category of materials.

Here is another example:

> The **textbooks** for my chemistry class are really expensive.
> **Textbooks** are really expensive.

In the first sentence, the noun *textbooks* refers only to the textbooks required for the speaker's chemistry class. However, in the second sentence, the speaker is using the noun *textbooks* in a completely different way: to make a generalization about the category of textbooks as a whole, not any particular group of textbooks.

We often use noncount nouns and plural count nouns without articles or other determiners in a second way: to identify a particular category of things (as opposed to other comparable categories), but not with the intention of generalizing about them. For example, a traffic sign may use a plural count noun to identify a category:

> The speed limit for **trucks** is 65 miles per hour.

The sign identifies a category of vehicles (*trucks*) without any further generalization about the nature of all trucks.

In the space provided after the sentence, identify the nouns in bold as either categorical or noncategorical. The first two questions are done as examples:

I think that **airports** are getting more crowded every day.   *categorical*

All the **airports** near us are impossibly crowded.   *noncategorical*

1. At midday, some **sunshine** was getting through the clouds. _____

2. **Sunshine** had bleached the old curtains until they were nearly white. _____

3. **Bridges** are always the most expensive part of road building. _____

4. The instructor said that **assignments** were due every Monday. _____

5. I couldn't finish the last **assignment**. _____

6. **Engines** often overheat on long trips through the desert. _____

7. In real estate, **location** is everything. _____

8. The company was looking for a new **location** for the plant. _____

9. There is a **freeze** on new hiring. _____

10. Success has a thousand fathers, while **failure** is an orphan. _____

Recognizing when nouns are being used to make categorical statements is key to using articles correctly. Here are two important characteristics of sentences that will help you recognize categorical statements:

1. **Present tense.** Categorical statements are almost always in the present tense because the present tense in English (unlike many languages) is essentially timeless. It is the tense we use to make generalizations. Accordingly, categorical statements will normally be in the simple present, the present progressive, or the present perfect. For example:

Noncount nouns

Present	**Depression** is a mental illness.
Present progressive	**Depression** is getting more common in young children.
Present perfect	**Depression** has become a major health issue.

Plural count nouns

Present	**Cherries** are in season now.
Present progressive	**Cherries** are getting popular as a health food.
Present perfect	**Cherries** have become more expensive.

2. **Adverbs of frequency.** Sentences that contain categorical statements often use adverbs of frequency such as the following: *always, generally, frequently, often,* and *usually,* plus the negative adverbs *rarely* and *never.* Note the underlined adverbs of frequency in the following sentences with categorical statements:

Noncount nouns

Comedy <u>always</u> gets a bigger audience than tragedy.
Criticism is <u>rarely</u> welcomed by the recipient.

Plural count nouns

Highways are <u>usually</u> maintained by gas taxes.
Mosquitoes are <u>frequently</u> a problem during the cooler parts of the day.

EXERCISE
3·7

If a noun is categorical put a ∅ in the space in front of the noun. If a noun is an indefinite noncategorical noun, put the appropriate article a/an or some in the blank space. (Note: For the purpose of this exercise, we will ignore the definite article the.) The first two questions have been done for you.

Getting enough _____∅_____ **rest** is a big problem when I travel.

Did you get _____*an*_____ **e-mail** from Louise?

1. We need _____ **answer** as soon as possible.

2. I have completely stopped eating _____ **cheese** because it has so many calories.

3. I had to throw _____ **cheese** away because it had gotten moldy.

4. _____ **live performances** are always more exciting than studio recordings.

5. _____ **TV channels** came in quite clearly.

6. I have always loved _____ **traveling**.

7. _____ **conferences** are always held in the spring and fall.

8. We eliminated _____ **locations** as unsuitable.

9. _____ **sea birds** rarely migrate.

10. Could you get me _____ **glass** of water, please?

Summary: Choosing the right article

Anytime you use an article with a common noun in English, you must make some complicated decisions in order to pick the right one. You must take into consideration two things:

1. **The WAY the article is being used.** Is the article being used to signal that the noun is **known to the hearer** (definite article *the*); that the noun is **not known to the hearer** (the indefinite articles *a/an* or *some*); or that the noun is being used to make a **categorical statement** (no article)?

2. **The TYPE of noun it is.** Is it a **singular count**, a **plural count**, or a **noncount** noun?

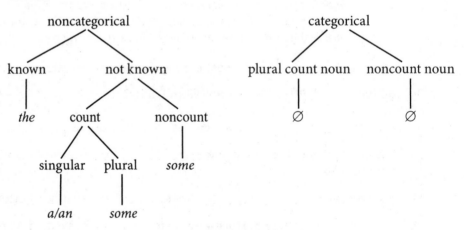

Quantifiers

The term *quantifier* refers to a number of pre-adjective noun modifiers (meaning they are placed before any adjectives) that express amount or degree. This section refers only to three sets of quantifiers that are affected by whether the noun being modified is count or noncount:

1. *many / much (a lot of)*

2. *few / little*

3. *fewer / less*

Many / much (a lot of)

Many is used only with plural count nouns; *much* is used only with noncount nouns:

Plural count nouns

His proposal has raised **many** issues.
There were **many** magazines in the doctor's office.

Many can be used in both questions and negative statements:

Questions

Did his proposal raise **many** issues?
Were there **many** magazines in the doctor's office?

Negative statements

His proposal did not raise **many** issues.
There were not **many** magazines in the doctor's office.

Noncount nouns

There has been **much** confusion about the time of the meeting.
It took **much** effort to finish the job on time.

While *much* is grammatical in positive statements, it often has an overly formal, old-fashioned feeling to it. In conversation, native speakers are much more likely to use *a lot of* instead of *much* in positive statements:

There has been **a lot of** confusion about the time of the meeting.
It took **a lot of** effort to finish the job on time.

In questions and negative statements, *much* and *a lot of* are used interchangeably:

Questions

Has there been **much / a lot of** confusion about the time of the meeting?
Did it take **much / a lot of** effort to finish the job on time?

Negative statements

There hasn't been **much / a lot of** confusion about the time of the meeting.
It didn't take **much/ a lot of** effort to finish the job.

EXERCISE

3·8

Fill in the blanks with many or much. *In positive statements, use* a lot of *instead of* much *when modifying noncount nouns. The first question is done as an example.*

Is there _____ *much* _____ information about this on the Web?

1. We didn't see _____ ducks on the pond.

2. We don't have _____ coffee left.

3. Not _____ high schools have tennis teams anymore.

4. There are _____ flu cases going around this winter.

5. I don't have _____ patience with his problems.

6. The garage doesn't keep _____ replacement parts on hand.

7. Do you get _____ snow in the winter?

8. Their actions have caused _____ grief for everyone.

9. We need to focus. There isn't _____ time.

10. There is _____ concern about this issue.

Few / little

Few is used only with plural count nouns; *little* is used only with noncount nouns:

Plural count nouns

Few mosquitoes around here carry malaria.
Few computers have adequate protection from spam.

Noncount nouns

We have had **little** information about what happened.
There was **little** public notice of the government's action.

However, for both plural count and noncount nouns, we normally use *any* rather than either *few* or *little* in questions and negative statements:

Questions

Do **any** mosquitoes around here carry malaria?
Do **any** computers have adequate protection from spam?

Negative statements

We have not had **any** information about what happened.
There wasn't **any** public notice of the government's action.

EXERCISE

3·9

Fill in the blanks with few *or* little *as appropriate in positive statements. Use* any *for questions and negative statements. The first question is done as an example.*

It was pretty late, so _____ *few* _____ cars were on the road.

1. The medication provided _____ relief from the pain.

2. Are _____ judges up for reelection this year?

3. _____ buildings had been damaged in the earthquake.

4. I had _____ confidence in the outcome of the election.

5. We didn't have _____ food left over after the picnic.

6. Please don't take _____ pictures during the performance.

7. Unfortunately, there is _____ assistance for the handicapped at the site.

8. We were delayed because there weren't _____ pilots available for our flight.

9. I took _____ pride in the way I behaved.

10. Are there _____ messages for me?

Fewer / less

Like *few* and *little*, the comparative form *fewer* is used with plural count nouns and *less* is used with noncount nouns:

Plural count nouns

Barbara is raising **fewer** sheep this year.
They are spending **fewer** summers at the lake than they used to.

Noncount nouns

There is **less** traffic on the roads since the rail line was opened.
He lost **less** weight this week.

However, unlike *few* and *little*, both *fewer* and *less* can be used in questions and negative statements. Their usage depends on whether they modify count or noncount nouns:

Questions

Is Barbara raising **fewer** sheep this year?
Are they spending **fewer** summers at the lake than they used to?
Is there **less** traffic on the roads since the rail line was opened?
Did he lose **less** weight this week?

Negative statements

Barbara is not raising **fewer** sheep this year.
They are not spending **fewer** summers at the lake than they used to.
There isn't **less** traffic on the roads since the rail line was opened.
He didn't lose **less** weight this week.

EXERCISE
3·10

Fill in the blanks with fewer *and* less *as appropriate. The first question is done as an example.*

Building the house took _____ *less* _____ lumber than we had expected.

1. There is _____ pressure in my new job.

2. The company has _____ job openings than before.

3. Does the revised plan have _____ floor space?

4. We don't have _____ paperwork than we did before we got computers.

5. There is _____ inflation than the government predicted.

6. _____ accidents mean lower insurance rates.

7. The side entryway has _____ steps to climb.

8. The job took _____ time than we had expected.

9. Smoking causes _____ deaths than before.

10. Since we remodeled, there is _____ light in the kitchen.

Adjectives

In this chapter we deal with two topics: (1) forming the comparative and superlative forms of adjectives, and (2) deriving adjectives from verb participles.

Forming the comparative and superlative forms of adjectives

The comparative and superlative forms of adjectives in English are unusual in that there are two different ways of forming them. One way uses the inflectional endings *-er* and *-est*. The other way uses the adverbs *more* and *most*. For example:

BASE FORM	COMPARATIVE FORM	SUPERLATIVE FORM
tall	taller	tallest
rude	ruder	rudest
beautiful	more beautiful	most beautiful
valuable	more valuable	most valuable

The reason English has two different ways of forming the comparative and superlative is historical. Modern English is a mixture of two different languages: Old English (Anglo-Saxon) and French. In Old English, all adjectives formed their comparative and superlative with *-er* and *-est*. The many hundreds of French adjectives that came into English in the Middle Ages tended to follow the French way of forming comparative and superlative by using adverbs, *more* and *most* in the case of English. Since most adjectives of Old English origin are one and two syllables and most adjectives of French origin are two, three, and even four syllables, people gradually came to associate length with the way of forming comparative and superlative forms regardless of historical origin: short words use *-er* and *-est*; long words use *more* and *most*. As a result, nearly all one-syllable adjectives in Modern English use *-er* and *-est* to form their comparative and superlative, and nearly all three- and four-syllable adjectives use *more* and *most*. The problem is that we cannot reliably predict how any particular two-syllable adjectives will form their comparative and superlative forms.

We can divide two-syllable adjectives into three groups: a large group that always uses *more/most*; a somewhat smaller second smaller group that can use either *more/most* or *-er/-est*; and a quite small third group that can only use *-er/-est*.

Two-syllable adjectives that always use *more/most*

This is by far the largest group. If you are not sure which form of the comparative and superlative to use, your best bet is always *more/most*. Here are some characteristics of the adjectives in this group:

Nearly all two-syllable adjectives that consist of only a single word part (i.e., not built with a stem + a suffix like, for example, *lonely*) must use *more/most*. For example:

BASE	COMPARATIVE	SUPERLATIVE
civil	more civil	most civil
modern	more modern	most modern
recent	more recent	most recent

Two-syllable adjectives made up of a certain stem + a suffix or inflectional ending also must use *more/most*.

Two-syllable adjectives that use the suffixes *-ful* and *-less* use *more/most*. For example:

| careful | more careful | most careful |
| hopeless | more hopeless | most hopeless |

Two-syllable adjectives ending in *-ed* or *-ing* that are derived from verbs must use *more/most*. For example:

amused	more amused	most amused
amusing	more amusing	most amusing
trusted	more trusted	most trusted
trusting	more trusting	most trusting

Two-syllable adjectives that can be used with either *more/most* or *-er/-est*.

The majority of adjectives in this group end in unstressed second syllables. The largest single group ends in *-ly*. For example:

	-ER/-EST	MORE/MOST
costly	costlier, costliest	more costly, most costly
deadly	deadlier, deadliest	more deadly, most deadly
lonely	lonelier, loneliest	more lonely, most lonely
ugly	uglier, ugliest	more ugly, most ugly

Note: The change of *y* to *i* follows the same spelling pattern we saw in the plural of nouns that end in *-y*. For example: *baby, babies; lady, ladies.*

Adjectives that end in unstressed vowels, *-er, -le, -el, -ere, -ure* can also use either pattern:

	-ER/-EST	MORE/MOST
mellow	mellower, mellowest	more mellow, most mellow
slender	slenderer, slenderest	more slender, most slender
gentle	gentler, gentlest	more gentle, most gentle
severe	severer, severest	more severe, most severe
obscure	obscurer, obscurest	more obscure, most obscure

Two-syllable adjectives that can only use *-er/-est*.

The largest group in this category ends in unstressed *-y*. For example:

BASE	COMPARATIVE	SUPERLATIVE
early	earlier	earliest
happy	happier	happiest
noisy	noisier	noisiest

Another group has the meaning of "small." There is something semantically inconsistent with using *more* and *most* with these words. For example:

> X I would like something <u>more little</u>.
> X I ended up buying <u>the most little</u> rug.

These words use *-er/-est*:

> I would like something <u>littler</u>.
> I ended up buying <u>the littlest</u> rug.

Write the comparative and superlative forms of the following two-syllable adjectives in the appropriate column. The first question is done as an example.

	MORE/MOST ONLY	MORE/MOST	-ER/-EST	-ER/-EST ONLY
	noble	more noble, most noble	nobler, noblest	
1. ancient	_____	_____	_____	_____
2. modern	_____	_____	_____	_____
3. silly	_____	_____	_____	_____
4. civil	_____	_____	_____	_____
5. friendly	_____	_____	_____	_____
6. ready	_____	_____	_____	_____
7. common	_____	_____	_____	_____
8. dreadful	_____	_____	_____	_____
9. shallow	_____	_____	_____	_____
10. mindless	_____	_____	_____	_____
11. private	_____	_____	_____	_____
12. recent	_____	_____	_____	_____
13. sincere	_____	_____	_____	_____
14. tiring	_____	_____	_____	_____
15. easy	_____	_____	_____	_____

Deriving adjectives from verb participles

Most languages form adjectives from verb participles. English is somewhat unusual because it uses both the present participle and the past participle to form adjectives. Here are some adjectives derived from present and past participles:

PRESENT PARTICIPLE	PAST PARTICIPLE
amusing	amused
charming	charmed
trusting	trusted

The adjectives derived from present participles and the adjectives derived from past participles have quite different meanings. For example, compare the following two sentences:

Present participle	Mr. Smith is a **boring** teacher.
Past participle	Mr. Smith is a **bored** teacher.

In the first example, the present participle adjective tells us that Mr. Smith bores his students. In the second example, the past participle tells us the exact opposite: Mr. Smith's students bore him.

These two participles have such dramatically different meanings because the participles maintain the different relationships that the underlying verb *bore* has with the noun *teacher*.

In the case of the present participle, the noun being modified, *teacher*, functions as the SUBJECT of the underlying verb *bore*. In other words, the teacher is doing the boring:

Present participle	Mr. Smith is a **boring teacher.**
	verb subject

In the case of the past participle, the noun being modified, *teacher,* functions as the OBJECT of the underlying verb *bore*. In other words, something or someone (his students presumably) is boring the teacher:

Past participle	Mr. Smith is a **bored teacher**.
	verb object

To correctly use present and past participles as adjectives, you must ask yourself whether the noun being modified is the subject, the "doer" of the action of the verb underlying the participle, or the object, the "recipient" of the action of the verb underling the participle.

Here are some more examples.

> After their (thrilling/thrilled) ride, the children could talk of nothing else.

What is the relationship of the noun being modified, *ride*, to the verb underlying the participles? Did the ride (subject) thrill the children, or did the children thrill the ride (object)? Once you consciously ask the question, the answer is obvious. The ride is the subject of the verb; the ride is doing the thrilling. Accordingly, we must use the present participle:

> After their **thrilling** ride, the children could talk of nothing else.

> Be sure you take the (prescribing/prescribed) amount of medicine.

Does the noun being modified, *amount of medicine*, do the prescribing (subject), or does someone (a doctor or pharmacist) prescribe the amount of medicine (object)? Clearly, the noun being modified is the object of the underlying verb. Accordingly, we must use the past participle:

> Be sure you take the **prescribed** amount of medicine.

The simplest way to decide which participle form to use is to see if you can use the noun being modified as the subject of an *-ing* form of the verb underlying the participle. If you can, use the present participle. If you cannot, use the past participle.

Here are some examples of the *-ing* test applied to two new examples:

> The new bridge is an (amazing/amazed) structure.

Ask yourself this question: is the structure amazing us? The answer is yes, so we know we should use the present participle form *amazing*:

> The new bridge is an **amazing** structure.

> She proudly waved her newly (issuing/issued) passport.

Ask yourself this question: is the passport issuing something? The answer is no, so we know we should use the past participle form *issued*:

> She proudly waved her newly **issued** passport.

Using the -ing test to pick the right form of the participle, cross out the wrong choice and underline the correct one. The first question is done as an example.

We went to a (<u>charming</u>/~~charmed~~) children's recital.

1. The (discouraging/discouraged) team left the field.

2. It was a very (tempting/tempted) offer.

3. Please play the (recording/recorded) message again.

4. We bought a new (recording/recorded) machine.

5. Her mother was a (respecting/respected) lawyer in the city.

6. The movie is set on a (deserting/deserted) island.

7. He gave a very (moving/moved) speech.

8. The Russians quickly followed Napoleon's (retreating/retreated) army.

9. Please stay out of the (restricting/restricted) area.

10. The new design incorporates many features of the (existing/existed) building.

11. The company fired the (striking/struck) employees.

12. We had to replace the (damaging/damaged) curtains.

13. We waived down a (passing/passed) taxi.

14. We got back a very (encouraging/encouraged) response.

15. The (attempting/attempted) coup failed miserably.

Verb forms and tenses ·5·

In this chapter we will examine the six basic verb forms of English and then explore the three rules that govern how these six verb forms are combined to create twelve verb constructions.

All verbs in English (with the important exception of the modal auxiliary verbs, which are discussed later in this chapter) have six forms: **base form, present tense, past tense, infinitive, present participle,** and **past participle**. The six forms are illustrated below using the regular verb *talk* and the irregular verb *sing*.

Verb forms

BASE FORM	PRESENT TENSE	PAST TENSE	INFINITIVE	PRESENT PARTICIPLE	PAST PARTICIPLE
talk	talk / talks	talked	to talk	talking	talked
sing	sing / sings	sang	to sing	singing	sung

Note that two forms of the verb *sing,* the past tense form *sang* and the past participle form *sung,* are in boxes. The past tense and the past participle forms of irregular verbs are unique in that they cannot be predicted by knowing the base form. All of the other forms are completely predictable from the base form.

The six forms of **base, present tense, past tense, infinitive, present participle**, and **past participle** are the building blocks that we use to make up all the verb constructions in English. These verb constructions are traditionally characterized as having nine different **tenses**. (We will see later why there are actually twelve different tenses.) These nine tenses are at the intersections of three **time** divisions (present, past, and future) and three **aspect** categories (simple, perfect, and progressive). The nine tenses arranged by time and aspect are given in the chart below, illustrated by the regular verb *talk* and the irregular verb *sing*:

The traditional nine tense constructions

	SIMPLE CATEGORY	PERFECT CATEGORY	PROGRESSIVE CATEGORY
Present time	he *talks*	he *has talked*	he *is talking*
	he *sings*	he *has sung*	he *is singing*
Past time	he *talked*	he *had talked*	he *was talking*
	he *sang*	he *had sung*	he *was singing*
Future time	he *will talk*	he *will have talked*	he *will be talking*
	he *will sing*	he *will have sung*	he *will be singing*

Note: *Will* is a member of a special group of five helping verbs called the **modal auxiliary verbs**. The five modal auxiliary verbs (along with their present and past tense forms) are given below:

MODAL	PRESENT TENSE	PAST TENSE
can	can	could
may	may	might
must	must	——
shall	shall	should
will	will	would

The string of up to three verbs in a row looks quite complicated, but the entire verb system in English is governed by three rules:

Rule #1: The first verb, and only the first verb, is tensed

A **tensed verb** is a verb inflected for either present tense or past tense. Only a tensed verb can enter into a subject-verb relationship with the subject. This means, of course, that only the first verb exhibits subject-verb agreement. At first glance, the future tense would seem to be an exception, but it is not. For example, in the sequence *he will talk*, *will* is the present tense of the modal auxiliary verb *will*.

Look at the following sentence:

It **might rain** tomorrow.

Might is the past-tense form of *may*. Note that the terms *present tense* and *past tense* when applied to modal verbs refer only to the form of the verb, not the meaning. In general, the past-tense form models express a greater degree of doubt, uncertainty, or tentativeness than the present tense forms. For example, compare the following:

Present	We can go to a movie.
Past	We could go to a movie.

The sentence with the past-tense modal is much more tentative than the sentence with the present-tense modal. The meanings of the modal forms are discussed in detail in Chapter 8.

Rule #2: All verb constructions except for the simple present and simple past consist of two verb components

The first component is a specific helping verb, and the second component is a particular verb form. Both components are fixed according to the following formula:

HELPING VERB (IN SOME FORM) + SPECIFIC VERB FORM

Future tense	modal auxiliary verb + base form
Perfect tenses	*have* + past participle
Progressive tenses	*be* + present participle

Here are examples that illustrate each of these three verb constructions:

Future tense (present or past tense modal + base form)

Harry **will be** late.
She **might have** a test tomorrow in economics.
We **can do** that.
You **should**n't **worry** about it.

Perfect aspect (*have* in some form + past participle)

I **have been** sick lately. (present perfect)
He **had run** all the way from the train station. (past perfect)
I **will have worked** here for ten years. (future perfect)

Progressive aspect (*be* in some form + present participle)

We **are working** late tonight. (present progressive)
I **was wondering** about that. (past progressive)
John **will be returning** from Los Angeles tomorrow. (future progressive)

Add either the perfect or progressive aspects to the following sentences as directed. Remember to keep the tense the same: a simple past will become a past perfect, and so forth. The first question is done as an example.

Bob **slept** all through the program. (perfect)

   Bob had slept all through the program.

1. We **will clean** the rooms tomorrow. (progressive)

   _____

2. We **stay** with the Joneses often. (perfect)

   _____

3. We **attracted** a crowd. (progressive)

   _____

4. They **will expand** the plant in Malaysia. (progressive)

   _____

5. We **adopted** a new policy. (perfect)

   _____

6. They **will emerge** from bankruptcy later this year. (progressive)

   _____

7. FedEx **should deliver** a package to you this morning. (progressive)

   _____

8. You **might hear** about a problem we've been having. (perfect)

   _____

9. They **threaten** to go to court. (progressive)

   _____

10. The spectators **could**n't **see** what actually happened. (perfect)

   _____

The traditional chart on page 52 is very misleading in one respect: the chart implies that the perfect and progressive aspects are mutually exclusive. In fact, sentences can be BOTH perfect AND progressive. (This accounts for the extra three verb constructions.) The perfect and progressive aspects are combined according to the following rule:

Rule #3: If both the perfect and the progressive aspects are used in the same verb sequence, the perfect always comes first

When this happens, the helping verb *have* (in whatever form it occurs) must be followed by the past participle *been*, which is the required helping verb for the progressive. At the same time, *been* functions as the helping verb for the progressive. In other words, the perfect and progressive overlap: the second element of the perfect (the verb *be* in the past participle form) is also the first element of the progressive. In all cases, the helping verb *been* must be followed by the main verb in the present participle form. For example:

Rain clouds **have been gathering** on the western horizon all morning.

have **been**
perfect

been gathering
progressive

This representation shows how *been* plays a double role: it is the second verb in the perfect construction and the first verb in the progressive construction at the same time. In this example the helping verb *have* is in the present tense, so the entire construction is a **present perfect progressive**.

Here are three more examples of sentences that include both the perfect and the progressive:

I **had been leaving** the mail on his desk while he was on vacation.

Comment: *had been* is in the perfect aspect; *been leaving* is in the progressive aspect.

Since the first verb *had* is in the past tense, the entire construction is thus a **past perfect progressive.**

She **has been advising** the new students all afternoon.

Comment: *has been* is in the perfect aspect; *been advising* is in the progressive aspect.

Since the first verb *has* is in the present tense, the entire construction is thus a **present perfect progressive.**

> They **will have been traveling** for two weeks now.

Comment: *will have been* is in the perfect aspect; *been traveling* is in the progressive aspect.

Since the first verb *will have* is in the future tense, the entire construction is thus a **future perfect progressive.**

The main verb in a verb sequence can also be *have*, resulting in two uses of the verb *have*, the first as a helping verb and the second as a main verb. For example:

> John **has been having** a lot of trouble with his knees lately.
>   helping   main
> We **had been having** some friends over when the fire broke out.
>   helping   main

Be can also be used as a main verb with the perfect and progressive. The result is a somewhat awkward combination of two uses of the verb *be* back to back. For example:

> The kids **have been being** cooperative all evening.
>   helping main
>
> Bobby **has been being** a pest ever since he came over.
>   helping   main

You will hear this construction in casual conversation, but it is usually avoided in writing and formal conversation.

EXERCISE
5·2

Add both the perfect and the progressive to the following sentences with simple verbs. Be sure to keep the tense the same. The first question is done as an example.

They **should keep** us informed.

> *They should have been keeping us informed.*

1. They **proposed** some important changes to the city charter.

_____

2. The drought **affects** local agriculture.

_____

3. They **will claim** damages resulting from the accident.

_____

4. We **repaired** the deck all afternoon.

_____

5. The company **issued** new stock recently.

_____

6. They **have** a lot of visitors lately.

_____

7. Everyone **hoped** to go on a picnic.

_____

8. They **should prepare** better.

_____

9. His parents **might stay** with them.

_____

10. We **have** too many false alarms lately.

_____

To summarize: the left-to-right order of even the most complicated verb construction is completely determined by a set of three rules that produce the following result:

1. The tensed verb comes first.

2. All verb constructions except for the simple present and simple past consist of two verb components. The first component is a specific helping verb, and the

second component is a particular verb form. All helping verbs control the form of the immediately following verb:

♦ Modals must be followed by a base form, creating the **future tenses**.

♦ *Have* must be followed by a past participle, creating the **perfect tenses**.

♦ *Be* must be followed by a present participle, creating the **progressive tenses**.

3. The perfect always comes before the progressive.

These rules will enable you to correctly identify the name of any verb construction in English (except for passives, which we will deal with later). Here is a set of examples showing the names for all twelve possible constructions:

Simple present	John **loses** his keys all the time.
Simple past	John **lost** his keys.
Simple future	John **will/could lose** his keys if he is not careful.
Present perfect	John **has lost** his keys again.
Past perfect	John **had lost** his keys in the parking lot, but soon found them.
Future perfect	John **may/might have lost** his keys again.
Present progressive	John **is** always **losing** his keys.
Past progressive	John **was** always **losing** his keys.
Future progressive	John **will/could be losing** his keys againif he isn't more careful.
Present perfect progressive	John **has been losing** his keys a lot lately.
Past perfect progressive	John **had been losing** his keys until he got a new keychain.
Future perfect progressive	John **may/could have been losing** his keys on purpose.

EXERCISE
5·3

Using the twelve names given above, write the name of each construction in the space provided under the sentence. The first question is done as an example.

Harry **was returning** from work when he got the message.

_____ past progressive _____

1. **Are** you **expecting** anyone?

_____

2. We **have spoken** before.

_____

3. **Should** they **be parking** on the grass?

_____

4. They **had** already **been rewriting** the contract all week.

_____

5. **Will** you **be staying** long?

_____

6. It **looks** good to me.

_____

7. We **will have been walking** for hours by the time we get home.

_____

8. I'**ve had** it!

_____

9. **Have** you **been listening** to anything I've said?

_____

10. She **will be taking** the late flight.

_____

The rules that govern the left-to-right order of English verb constructions is so deterministic that you can actually scramble the word order of the verbs and still figure out what the order must be. For example:

> X You **suggested have should** that they start sooner.

First, look at each of the verbs in their existing left-to-right order:

- ◆ _Suggested_ can be either a past tense or a past participle.
- ◆ _Have_ is an infinitive.
- ◆ _Should_ is a past-tense modal.

We know that the modal must come first (since a modal is ALWAYS a tense-carrying verb) (Rule #1) and that the modal must be followed immediately by a base-form verb (Rule #2), and the only base-form verb is *have*. That means the first two verbs are *should have*. Since the modal *should* is a tensed verb (and there can only be one tensed verb in any verb construction), we know that *suggested* cannot be a past tense; *suggested* must therefore be a past participle following the helping verb *have* (Rule #2). The only possible sequence is the following:

should have suggested

This construction is a **future perfect**.

EXERCISE
5·4

The verbs in bold have been scrambled. Write the verbs in the only possible correct order and give the name of the tense in parentheses. The first question is done as an example.

The new teacher **using had been** the wrong textbook.

_____ *had been using* _____   _____ *past perfect progressive)* _____

1. You **have been should** more careful.

_____   _____

2. The program **continuing be will** next year.

_____   _____

3. We **have been must** mistaken.

_____   _____

4. I **hearing have been** good things about your work.

_____   _____

5. They **talking be must** to each other.

_____   _____

6. We **have having been** a very warm summer this year.

_____   _____

7. The students **been have should studying** financial management.

_____   _____

8. You **working been have** too hard.

_____   _____

9. We **had have should** a break by now.

_____   _____

10. I **being been might have** out of line lately.

_____   _____

Talking about present time

In this chapter we will examine the many and complicated ways that English uses to talk about present time. We will focus on (1) the present and present progressive tenses, and (2) the present perfect tense.

The present and present progressive tenses

On the face of it, talking about present time seems obvious: just use the present tense. The problem is that the present tense does not really mean present time as we would define it logically as the present moment or point in time. Instead, the English verb system looks at present time in a different way. Present time is an ongoing existing state.

If we want to express that an action is specific to the present moment in time, we don't use the present tense at all: instead we use the **present progressive**. For example, compare the following sentences, the first in the present tense, the second in the present progressive:

Present tense	Bob's sister **lives** on Elm Street.
Present progressive	Bob's sister **is living** on Elm Street.

The use of the present tense in the first sentence tells us that Bob's sister has lived on Elm Street for some time and plans to continue living on Elm Street for a while—the ongoing existing state. The use of the present tense does not mean that she is there at this particular moment. In fact, she could have been away in Florida for the entire winter. In other words, the present tense signals an ongoing, existing, or habitual state, but says nothing about the present moment in time.

The use of the present progressive in the second sentence indicates something else: Bob's sister is living on Elm Street right now at this moment, but either she has not lived there long or she is planning to move, or both. In other words, the present progressive signals that the action is tied to a particular, limited moment in time and is, therefore, temporary.

The moment in time, however, can be quite lengthy. For example:

> Louise **is studying** economics at Berkeley this year.

Even though a year is a long time, the use of the present progressive signals that the speaker views Louise's stay in Berkeley as a time-limited (and thus momentary) event. The speaker did not have to set a limit on Louise's time in Berkeley, as in the following example:

> Louise **is studying** economics at Berkeley.

The use of the present progressive means that the speaker views Louise's stay in Berkeley as temporary.

EXERCISE 6·1

Each of the following sentences indicates whether the action is an ongoing state or is momentary. Use the present or present progressive of the base-form verb in bold as appropriate. The first question is done as an example.

Momentary   I **handle** the situation as best I can.

    I am handling the situation as best I can.

1. *Ongoing state*   She **miss** her old school.

   _____

2. *Momentary*   You **miss** the point.

   _____

3. *Momentary*   He **avoid** crowds during the flu season.

   _____

4. *Ongoing state*   Her company **publish** science and medical textbooks.

   _____

5. *Momentary*   She **teach** Econ 101 this semester.

   _____

6. *Ongoing state*   He always **enjoy** a glass of wine with dinner.

   _____

7. *Momentary*   I **come** down with a cold.

_____

8. *Momentary*   We **think** about moving to Florida.

_____

9. *Ongoing*   He always **put** on a tie when he goes out to dinner.

_____

10. *Momentary*   I **face** an important decision.

_____

The present tense is most commonly used for the following three purposes:

1. To state an objective fact (which, of course, may or may not be correct). For example:

> The sun **sets** at 6:35 tonight.
> Christmas **falls** on a Sunday this year.

2. To make an assertion, generalization, or observation. For example:

> The American diet **contains** far too much sugar and fat.
> The rug **needs** to be vacuumed.
> My knee always **hurts** when I walk too far.

3. To describe habitual or repeated actions. For example:

> I **call** my mom every Sunday.
> They **go** skiing nearly every winter.
> We **stay** with friends whenever we are in town.

*In each of the following sentences, a present-tense verb in bold is correctly used. For each present-tense verb, indicate which of the three meanings of the present tense best describes the meaning of this verb: **objective fact, assertion,** or **habitual action**. The first question is done as an example.*

I always **allow** a few extra minutes when I take the train. _____*habitual*_____

1. Exercise **reduces** the risk of heart disease. _____

_____

2. The moon **determines** the rise and fall of the tides. _____

_____

3. Health insurance **costs** too much. _____

_____

4. We always **get** popcorn when we go to the movies. _____

_____

5. Water **covers** 80 percent of the earth's surface. _____

_____

6. In Japan they **drive** on the left side of the road. _____

_____

7. People seldom **save** enough for their retirement. _____

_____

8. The recent increase in inflation **proves** that the government is spending too

much. _____

_____

9. Every night we **watch** a little TV before we go to bed. _____

_____

10. A decision by the supreme court **binds** all decisions by lower courts. _____

_____

While most verbs can be used in either the present tense or the present perfect tense depending on the situation, a number of verbs in English are not normally used in the progressive tenses. These verbs are called **stative** verbs. To see the difference between normal verbs (nonstative) and stative verbs, compare the following sentences with the verbs *drive* and *own*:

Nonstative verb	Harry **drives** a red convertible.
	Harry **is driving** a red convertible.
Stative verb	Harry **owns** a red convertible.
	X Harry **is owning** a red convertible.

The verb *drive* shows the normal distinction between an ongoing state in the first example (present tense) and a temporary condition in the second example (present progressive). In other words, the verb *drive* can be used either way depending on the situation and the speaker's intention.

The verb *own*, however, is different. English treats all verbs of possession as inherently being in an ongoing state. Accordingly, they cannot normally be used in the progressive tenses. The use of the progressive with the stative verb *own* is ungrammatical. Using the progressive tenses with stative verbs is a very common error that even advanced nonnative speakers make.

Most stative verbs fall into the following three semantic categories (with examples):

Mental activity or state: *believe, doubt, imagine, know, mean*

I **believe** that you are right.
X I **am believing** that you are right.

Emotional condition: *appreciate, care, envy, fear, hate, like, love, prefer, want*

I **appreciate** your help.
X I **am appreciating** your help.

Possession: *belong, consist of, contain, hold, own, possess*

That house **belongs** to my parents.
X That house **is belonging** to my parents.

Some verbs can be used as either stative or nonstative verbs, but with a difference in meaning. For example the verb *care* in the sense of "being concerned" is stative, but in the sense of "tend or take care of" it is nonstative:

Stative	I **care** what you think.
	X I **am caring** what you think.
Nonstative	I **care** for my sister's pets whenever she is out of town.
	I **am caring** for my sister's pets all this week.

Sometimes native speakers deliberately use a stative verb in a progressive tense for extra emphasis. Advertisers deliberately misuse stative verbs to get our attention. For example, here is a recent ad for McDonald's:

I'm loving it!

Since we would normally say *I love it*, the use of the progressive makes us notice the ad.

EXERCISE
6·3

Replace the present-tense verbs in bold with the present progressive, UNLESS the verb is a stative verb. In that case, write "stative" on the line. The first two questions are done as examples.

This paint **dries** too quickly.

This paint ~~dries~~ too quickly. _____*is drying*_____

I **prefer** my coffee with cream.

I **prefer** my coffee with cream. _____*Stative*_____

1. I **count** to ten. _____

   _____

2. He **dislikes** having to repeat himself. _____

   _____

3. The rebel advance **threatens** the capital. _____

   _____

4. We **want** to leave after work as soon as we can. _____

   _____

5. The boss always **finds** more jobs for us to do. _____

_____

6. The office **examines** everyone's expense account. _____

_____

7. Our stock portfolio **consists** of bonds. _____

_____

8. The publisher **reviews** her latest book. _____

_____

9. Our pool **contains** 5,000 gallons of water. _____

_____

10. I **know** what you mean! _____

_____

We also use the present tense for certain kinds of narratives or descriptions that really stand outside of time. The most common of these are reviews or reports, or when summarizing the words of someone else. Here are some examples:

Review: The 1975 Australian movie *Picnic at Hanging Rock* **tells** of the mysterious disappearance of three schoolchildren and their teacher on a school outing in the Australian Bush in 1900. Four children **wander** away from the main group. One of the teachers **goes** to search for them and also **disappears**. . . .

Report: The 401(k) plans of comparable midsized companies **allow** employees almost total freedom to invest in any way they **see** fit. Most employees, however, **opt** to use whatever default investment that **is** created by the employer. Sometimes these default investments **are** not well suited to the individual needs of the employee. . . .

Summary: Our current policy manual **gives** first-year salaried employees two weeks of paid leave annually. The amount of paid leave **rises** with seniority to a maximum of three weeks' vacation. The policy manual **does** not distinguish between vacation time, sick leave, or leave for family emergencies. . . .

We also use the present tense in casual conversation for telling jokes. For example:

This guy **goes** into a bar and **sees** a kangaroo drinking a fancy mixed drink with a little umbrella in it. He **walks** up to the kangaroo and **says**, "We **don't** see many talking kangaroos in here." The kangaroo **replies**, "Well, at these prices, I**'m** not surprised."

The following sentences all use the present tense in an unusual way. If the present tense is used for talking about the foreseeable future, write "future." If the present tense is used for narrative, write "narrative." The first two questions are done as examples.

The plot of the movie **seems** somewhat artificial. _____*narrative*_____

The play **gets** over at 10:15. _____*future*_____

1. Section 312 clearly **states** eligibility for overtime pay. _____

2. The book **begins** with the discovery of gold at Sutter's Mill in 1849. _____

3. The cafeteria **closes** today at 5:00. _____

4. The play **ends** with the Prince calling for the families to reconcile. _____

5. All major decisions of the CEO **are** submitted to the board for approval. _____

6. We **spend** Christmas with my husband's family this year. _____

7. In case of a major accident involving hazardous materials, the police **close** the freeway to all traffic. _____

8. Our wake-up call **is** at 6:30 tomorrow morning. _____

9. In 1959, Hawaii **is** admitted to the Union as the fiftieth state. _____

_____

10. The sun **sets** around 8:00 on Saturday. _____

_____

The present perfect tense

The present perfect consists of the helping verb *have* (in the present-tense form *has* or *have*) plus a following verb in the past participle form. The present perfect is used in several ways, but all of these uses share this core meaning: the present perfect describes actions or conditions that began at some point in the past and that have continued in an unbroken, continuous, repeated, or habitual manner up to the present moment of time. Here are some examples that illustrate this basic meaning:

> I **have known** him since we were in grade school.
> She **has** always **lived** in Los Angles.
> We **have shopped** at Ralph's grocery store for years.

The present perfect focuses on what has happened up to the present moment in time with little or no implication about the future. In this respect, the present perfect is very different from the present tense. To see the difference, compare the following sentences:

> *Present perfect*   We **have lived** in River City for five years.
> *Present tense*   We **live** in River City.

The present perfect sentence focuses on the duration that the speaker has lived in River City. There is no implication that the speaker will continue to live there in the future (although that may be the case). In contrast, the sentence with the present tense strongly implies that the speaker will continue to live in River City into the future.

Notice that all the examples of the present perfect have an adverbial expression of duration. Here are the four examples with the expression of duration underlined:

> I **have known** him <u>since we were in grade school</u>.
> She **has** <u>always</u> **lived** in Los Angles.
> We **have shopped** at Ralph's grocery store <u>for years</u>.
> We **have lived** in River City <u>for five years</u>.

Unless there were some context that supplied an implied period of duration, these sentences would sound odd if the expressions of duration were deleted:

> ? I **have known** him.
> ? She **has lived** in Los Angles.
> ? We **have shopped** at Ralph's grocery store.
> ? We **have lived** in River City.

The present tense, however, is incompatible with an adverbial expression of duration. For example:

> X I **know** him <u>since we were in grade school.</u>
> X She <u>always</u> **lives** in Los Angeles.
> X We **shop** at Ralph's grocery store <u>for years.</u>
> X We **live** in River City <u>for five years.</u>

EXERCISE
6·5

The sentences below contain either a present-tense verb or a present perfect verb in bold. Following each sentence is an adverbial expression of duration in parenthesis. Add the adverbial expression to the appropriate place in the sentence if it is grammatically correct to do so. If it is grammatically incorrect to add the adverbial expression, write "ungrammatical." The first two questions are done as examples.

I **have driven** to that airport. (a hundred times)

> *I have driven to that airport a hundred times.*

I **work** near the airport. (for a couple of years)

> *ungrammatical*

1. He **stays** with some friends. (since Christmas)

2. They **have studied** together. (all this semester)

3. The company **has lost** money. (ever since the recession began)

4. The tomatoes **grow** rapidly. (since we started fertilized them)

_____

5. We **have discussed** our differences openly. (always)

_____

6. They **have worked** on the project. (ever since it was first approved)

_____

7. Senator Brown **fights** against corruption. (since she was first elected)

_____

8. He **suffers** a skin condition. (from childhood)

_____

9. She **is** away from home. (since she was seventeen)

_____

10. They **have argued** over it. (always)

_____

There are two other uses of the present perfect, neither of which requires an overt expression of duration. The most important of these uses describes an event or situation that has just occurred in the immediate past and that directly affects the present.

To see how this is different from the ordinary past tense, compare the following sentences:

Present perfect	Marvin **has lost** his keys.
Past tense	Marvin **lost** his keys.

The implication of the present perfect sentence is that Marvin's losing his keys directly affects the present moment. In fact, we should probably all help Marvin find his keys. On the other hand, the past-tense sentence is telling us something about a past event that has no implication for us in the present time. It is used for an event that is over and done with.

The immediacy of the present perfect is shown by the fact that we can use the adverb _just_ (which refers to something that happened only moments ago) with the present perfect, but not with the past tense. For example:

Present perfect	Marvin **has** just **lost** his keys.
Past tense	X Marvin just **lost** his keys yesterday.

As you might expect, we cannot use a past-time adverb *yesterday* with the present perfect, while it is perfectly normal with past tense. For example:

Present perfect	X Marvin **has lost** his keys <u>yesterday</u>.
Past tense	Marvin **lost** his keys <u>yesterday</u>.

The other use of the present perfect that does not require an adverbial phrase of duration has the meaning of "to do something or complete some action over a span of time before the present moment." For example:

Our son **has read** every one of the Harry Potter books.
We **have accumulated** nearly 100,000 frequent flyer miles.
How much money **have** you **saved**?

EXERCISE
6·6

All of the sentences below are in the present perfect. Identify which use of the present perfect best describes the sentence: (1) continuous activity, (2) immediate past action, or (3) completed action. The first question is done as an example.

Sherlock Holmes **has** just **discovered** the murderer.

   (2) immediate past action

1. He **has collected** every U.S. stamp issued before 1900.

   _____

2. She **has administered** the program for many years.

   _____

3. I **have** just **spoken** to the manager about the problem.

   _____

4. He **has fixed** that door a dozen times and it still sticks.

   _____

5. She **has** just **stepped** away from her desk and will be back in a minute.

   _____

6. They **have accomplished** the impossible.

_____

7. It **has rained** every weekend this summer.

_____

8. He **has kept** every penny he ever earned.

_____

9. I **have** repeatedly **urged** him to slow down when he drives through town.

_____

10. I **have** just **figured** out the answer.

_____

Talking about past time

After a brief discussion of a group of irregular verbs that forms its past tense and past participle in a unique way, this chapter examines in depth two ways of talking about the past: (1) the past tense, and (2) the past perfect tense.

While you have been studying lists of irregular verbs ever since you began studying English, there is a large group of irregular verbs that you are probably not even aware of. This group (which is the largest group of irregular verbs that follows the same pattern) is highly unusual in that it is mostly predictable IF you know what to look for. Twenty-four irregular verbs have past tense and past participles that are identical to their base forms. Here are two examples:

BASE FORM	PAST TENSE	PAST PARTICIPLE
put	put	put
wed	wed	wed

All twenty-four of the verbs in this group share the following characteristics:

1. The base form ends in either -t (like *put*) or -d (like *wed*).

2. The verbs are all single-syllable words.

3. The verbs are all pronounced with a short vowel.

4. With the exception of *hurt* three verbs that end in -st (*burst, cast, cost*) they do not end in final consonant clusters.

All verbs (and only those verbs) that meet the above four conditions have past tenses and past participles identical with their base forms. Here are some verbs ending in -t or -d that FAIL to meet these conditions:

> *submit* (more than one syllable)
> *eat* (long vowel)
> *build* (ends in a consonant cluster)

As we would predict, none of these three verbs has a past tense and a past participle that is identical with its infinitive:

BASE FORM	PAST TENSE	PAST PARTICIPLE
submit	submitted	submitted
eat	ate	eaten
build	built	built

Each question contains a list of four verbs that ends in either -t or -d. Only one of the four verbs meets the criteria and has a past tense and past participle form that is identical with the base form. The other three verbs fail one or more of the criteria and do NOT have past tenses and past participle forms that are identical with their base forms. Identify the one verb that meets the criteria. The first question is done as an example.

adopt, hit, meet, paint _____ *hit* _____

1. end, knit, limit, treat _____

2. bleed, cut, grant, yield _____

3. depend, fit, recommend, mount _____

4. attract, count, reflect, quit _____

5. defend, lend, let, visit _____

6. light, select, split, want _____

7. confront, insist, protect, shut _____

8. consult, promote, speed, wet _____

9. add, bid, need, test _____

10. bind, expand, present, rid _____

The past tense

The past tense is used to refer to events that were completed in the past. The past tense can refer to a single moment in past time. For example:

I **got** to the office a little after nine.

The past tense can refer to something that occurred repeatedly in the past. For example:

It **rained** every weekend this summer.

The past tense can refer to a span of past time. For example:

Jayne **worked** in Washington for about six years.

It is important to bear in mind that the span of time in the last example sentence has been completed before the present moment of time: Jayne no longer works in Washington.

The past tense is also used in two other ways: in hypothetical statements and to make polite requests. These two special uses of the past tense are survivals of the **subjunctive** verb form that once existed in earlier forms of English.

The most important of these past-tense subjunctives in modern English is to signal that the speaker is talking hypothetically or even contrary to fact. We most often see this kind of past-tense subjunctive in clauses that begin with *if*. For example:

If I **were** John, I would be careful what I said to the boss.

In this example, the speaker uses the past tense to signal to the audience that what is being said is hypothetical—the speaker knows full well that he is not John.

The *if* clause does not have to begin the sentence. It can follow the other clause. For example:

I would be careful what I said to the boss, if I **were** John.

Here are some more examples of past-tense subjunctives used in *if* clauses:

If you **were** in my shoes, what would you do?
If they **made** a mistake in calculating our expenses, we could be in trouble.
If I **said** something inappropriate, I apologize.

The other modern English use of the past-tense subjunctive is to show polite deference, especially in asking questions or making requests. For example, if you asked a colleague to do something, you would probably use the present tense:

Can you hold the elevator for a moment?

However, if you were asking your boss the same question, you would probably use the past-tense subjunctive:

Could you hold the elevator for a moment?

If you wanted to issue an invitation to a friend, you would probably use the present tense. For example:

Do you want to go get something to eat?

However, if a boy asked out a girl he did not know well, he would probably use the past-tense subjunctive:

Would you like to go get something to eat?

EXERCISE

7·2

All of the following sentences contain a past-tense verb in bold. Indicate which meaning the past tense has. If it is past time, write "past time." If it is hypothetical past-tense subjunctive, write "hypothetical." If is it polite past-tense subjunctive, write "polite." The first question is done as an example.

He would be really upset if we **were** to miss the meeting.   _hypothetical_

1. Who **turned** off the printer?   _____

2. **Could** you turn down the radio?   _____

3. I **graduated** in 2003.   _____

4. If it **were** up to me, I would work from home.   _____

5. I **did**n't get a chance to talk to him.   _____

6. **Did** you want to rest a minute before we go on?   _____

7. Unless I **got** a better offer, I would stay in my current job.   _____

8. We **concluded** that we are better off not doing anything.   _____

9. If I **quit** smoking, I could save a lot of money.   _____

10. **Could** you give me a minute to get ready?   _____

The past perfect tense

The past perfect tense consists of *had* (the past-tense form of the helping verb *have*) followed by a second verb in the past participle form. The event or action described in the past perfect tense must be completed prior to some more recent past-time event. The purpose of using the past perfect tense is to emphasize the relative sequence of two past-time events. Here are some examples.

> They **had** already **left** by the time we got back.
>   earlier event   later event
>
> The storm **had** already **passed** before we got to the campground.
>   earlier event   later event
>
> Just after I **had stepped** into shower, the phone rang.
>   earlier event   later event
>
> They **had lived** in Paris before the war.
>   earlier event   later event

One of the features of the past perfect that can make it difficult to use is that the two time events can appear in the sentence in either order. That is, the later event can precede the earlier event. Here are the same example sentences given above with the clauses in reverse order:

> By the time we got back, they **had** already **left**.
>   later event   earlier event
>
> Before we got to the campground, the storm **had** already **passed**.
>   later event   earlier event
>
> The phone rang just after I **had stepped** into the shower.
>   later event   earlier event
>
> Before the war, they **had lived** in Paris.
>   later event   earlier event

The past perfect is a difficult tense to use because it takes a certain amount of planning. For that reason, you will hear in casual conversation the simple past used where the past perfect should be used. For example:

> X They **got** into a big fight just before they **broke** up.

Notice that both clauses in this example are in the past tense. To correct the sentence, you have to decide which event occurred first and which occurred second. The use of *before* in the second clause tells us that (1) they got into a big fight first, and then (2) they broke up. (Cause and effect?) Here are the two possible forms of the corrected sentence:

> They **had gotten** into a big fight just before they broke up.
> Just before they broke up, they **had gotten** into a big fight.

Both clauses in the following sentences contain a past tense verb in bold. Draw a line through the verb that is incorrect and write the corrected past perfect tense. The first question is done as an example.

When we **bought** the house, it **was** empty for two years.

When we **bought** the house, it ~~was~~ empty for two years. _____*had been*_____

1. The storm **closed** the runways before we **were** cleared for takeoff. _____

2. When we **returned** from vacation, we found that our house **was** broken into. _____

   _____

3. We **had** to forfeit the game because we **used** an ineligible player. _____

4. We were **bumped** from the flight even though the airlines already **confirmed** our reservations. _____

5. Even before they **looked** at the house, they **made** a decision to buy it. _____

6. The office already **closed** before we **got** there. _____

7. Even before he **got** the check, Bobby already **spent** the money. _____

8. Fred's counselor **advised** him to change majors after she **looked** at Fred's grades.

   _____

9. After he **made** a big sale, he **was** promoted to the head of marketing. _____

10. We **pulled** over to the side of the road after the "check engine" light **came** on. _____

   _____

Talking about future time ·8·

This chapter focuses on the various ways English has developed for talking about the future. In particular we will examine (1) the modal auxiliary verbs, and (2) the present and present progressive tenses.

Talking about the future and planning for it are things that people love to discuss. Not surprisingly, then, English has developed a number of different ways to talk about the future. Unfortunately, English has not developed very good terminology for talking about these numerous options.

The first obstacle is the term **future tense** itself. English has never had a future tense in the sense that the Romance languages like Latin, French, Italian, and Spanish have. In those languages, there is a set of inflected forms of the verb that refers to future time. In the distant, prehistorical past, the Germanic ancestral language of English (as well as modern German, Dutch, and the Scandinavian languages) lost this entire set of future-tense inflections.

The probable reason for the disappearance of the future tense from all Germanic languages is that the ancestral Germanic language developed a suite of helping verbs that allows people to talk about the future in a very sophisticated way. These helping verbs, called **modal auxiliary verbs**, evidently proved so successful that they completely replaced the older future-tense inflectional system.

Here is the complete set of modal auxiliary verbs:

Modal auxiliary verbs

BASE FORM	PRESENT TENSE	PAST TENSE
can	can	could
may	may	might
must	must	
shall	shall	should
will	will	would

There are two big differences in form between modal and normal (i.e., nonmodal) verbs:

83

1. Modals do not have any infinitive, present participle, or past participle forms.

2. None of the present-tense modals has a third-person singular -*s*. (The historical reason for this odd fact is that all of the modern present-tense forms of modals were originally past-tense forms that never had the third-person singular -*s* to begin with. Over time all of the present-tense modals except *must* evolved new past-tense forms to replace the lost past-tense forms. *Must* is thus the only verb in English that does not have a past-tense form.)

The modals are always followed by a verb in its **base form**. A base-form verb is the dictionary-entry form of a verb. It is like an infinitive except it does not have *to* in front of the verb. This base-form verb must play one of the following three roles: the main verb, the helping verb *be* as part of the progressive tense, or the helping verb *have* as part of the perfect tense. For example:

Main verb

We will **let** you know.
You should **do** better next time.

Helping verb *be* followed by a present participle as part of a progressive tense

I will **be** seeing them this afternoon.
The kids should **be** doing their homework instead of watching TV.

Helping verb *have* followed by a past participle as part of a perfect tense

The class might **have** studied tenses already.
They should **have** finished by now.

Note: Both *be* and *have* can also be used as main verbs after a modal verb. For example:

Be as a main verb

We will **be** late for our meeting if we don't hurry.
I can't **be** everywhere at once.

Have as a main verb

I will **have** the pasta.
They can **have** as much time as they need.

Underline the base-form verb in the following sentences. Then identify the role that the base-form verb plays: (1) main verb, (2) helping verb as part of the progressive tense, or (3) helping verb as part of a perfect tense by writing "main verb," "progressive helping verb," or "perfect helping verb" in the space provided. The first question is done as an example.

I will not be working from home this week. _____

I will not <u>be</u> working from home this week _____*progressive helping verb*_____

1. We shouldn't fear the future. _____

2. They must have adjusted the height of the seat. _____

3. I'll have a soda, please. _____

4. She will be retiring in a couple of years. _____

5. The police must have noticed the broken window. _____

6. We will invite them to our next reception. _____

7. The meeting will be over by six at the latest. _____

8. We must be going soon. _____

9. The revisions will have cost us a fortune by the time we are done. _____

10. The wind might be dropping a little. _____

Another big difference between modal and regular verbs is that the terms **present tense** and **past tense** refer only to historical verb forms, not to time. The modals stand outside of the tense system: the present-tense modals do not refer to present time, nor do the past-tense modals refer to past time. The modals function as **subjunctive** verbs. Subjunctive verbs convey information about the possibility or probability of doing something or something happening, about the necessity or obligation of doing something or of something happening, about things that are hypothetical or an event contrary to fact.

Most uses of the nine modals fall into one of these five subjunctive categories:

1. **Prediction** of future activities and events

2. **Obligation** to carry out future activities or actions

3. **Necessity** of the occurrence of future events or actions

4. **Permission** or **request** to carry out a future actions

5. **Capability** of engaging in future actions

EXERCISE
8·2

Using one of the five categories above, pick the category (or sometimes two categories) that the modals in the following sentences best fit. The first question is done as an example.

We **shall** overcome. _____(3) prediction_____

1. It **may** rain tomorrow. _____

2. You **may** go to the party, but only if you are back before midnight. _____

3. You **can** do it! _____

4. The Cubs **might** actually finish in first place this year. _____

5. You **should** write them a thank-you note. _____

6. The company **should** start making money next year. _____

7. I **must** get to the office early tomorrow. _____

8. **Shall** we start now? _____

9. I **may** be able to help you. _____

10. They **won't** be ready until next week sometime. _____

While each of the nine modals has its own range of meanings, the past-tense modals all tend to have a hypothetical or tentative meaning. We saw this same subjunctive use of the past tense in Chapter 7, "Talking about past time," with the use of the past tense in *if* clauses. For example:

If I **were** you, I would not do that.

To see the typical difference between a present-tense modal and its past-tense counterpart, compare the following sentences:

| *Present tense* | We **can** meet at lunchtime. |
| *Past tense* | We **could** meet at lunchtime. |

The speakers in both sentences are making a suggestion. However, the sentences have very different implications. The speaker who used *can* is making a proposal that the speaker expects the listeners to accept or at the least offer an alternative. The speaker who used *could* is throwing out a much more tentative suggestion that invites discussion and even counterproposals.

EXERCISE
8·3

Pick the appropriate form of the pair of modals that best fits the meaning of the sentence and write it in the blank space within the sentence. The first question is done as an example.

may/might: We _____*might*_____ drop by after dinner, but it will probably be too late.

1. can/could: I have every confidence that you _____ do it.

2. shall/should: Electrical devices _____ meet legal standards wherever possible.

3. will/would: We _____ meet with the committee at nine tomorrow morning.

4. may/might: It _____ rain, but the weather looks pretty good now.

5. can/could: They _____ make the changes if it were absolutely necessary.

6. will/would: I _____ be happy to do it, if I had the time.

7. may/might: You _____ go outside and play now.

8. shall/should: Electrical devices _____ meet legal standards or the permit will be denied.

9. can/could: The animals _____ take care of themselves just fine.

10. will/would: We _____ keep at it until the job is done.

Using the present and present progressive tenses for future time

Both the present and present progressive tenses can be used to talk about the future, but in slightly different ways. The present tense is used for established events or events that are known or fixed. For example:

> Our flight **leaves** at 7:35.
> The moon **rises** at 6:44 this evening.
> The meeting **begins** at 2:30.

We use the present tense in questions when we ask for information that is already established or known (though not, of course, by the person asking the question). For example:

> When **does** the next train for Chicago leave?
> When **does** your school start this year?
> When **does** Ms. Kaufman get back from vacation?

Another way to think of the present tense is that it is used for information that is "old" in the sense that it is already fixed and known to others (though, again, not to the person asking the question).

The present progressive, on the other hand, is used for information that is not already established or not known by another member of the conversation. In that sense it is "new" information. Here is a typical situation in which the present progressive is appropriate and the present is ungrammatical.

Your immediate supervisor makes the following announcement to you and your colleagues: "Mr. Brown **is calling** a special meeting tomorrow at 4:00." The use of the present progressive signals that your supervisor knows that you and your colleagues could not have known or anticipated this new information. The use of the present tense instead of the present progressive for the same message would be ungrammatical: "X Mr. Brown **calls** a special meeting tomorrow at 4:00."

Here are some more example where the present progressive is grammatical but the present is not:

Present progressive	I **am** not **answering** any calls this afternoon.
Present	X I **do** not answer any calls this afternoon.
Present progressive	We **are going** back early, so get your coat.
Present	X We **go** back early, so get your coat.
Present progressive	I **am telling** my parents the good news when we see them.
Present	X I **tell** my parents the good news when we see them.

Neither tense can be used for unpredictable, unplanned future events. For example:

Present progressive   X The Yankees **are winning** tomorrow's game.
Present   X The Yankees **win** tomorrow's game.

Each of the following sentences has a blank space where the verb should go. In front of each sentence there are two verb forms in parentheses: the present and the present perfect. Pick which form best suits the meaning of the sentence and write it in the blank space. If neither one is appropriate, write "none." The first question is done as an example.

begins/is beginning: The play _____*begins*_____ promptly at eight.

1. drifts/is drifting: Fortunately, the storm _____ out to sea tonight.

2. comes/is coming: Due to an accident on the freeway, he _____ in late.

3. falls/is falling: Christmas _____ on a Saturday next year.

4. take/am taking: I won't be at the meeting Tuesday; I _____ the day off.

5. rains/is raining: It _____ tomorrow.

6. does the office open/is the office opening: When _____?

7. close/are closing: All the banks _____ at six today.

8. catch/are catching: They _____ the late flight tonight.

9. closes/is closing: The stock market _____ up tomorrow.

10. get/are getting: We _____ a pizza for dinner tonight.

Causative verbs

Causative verbs are verbs in which somebody (or something) causes somebody (or something) to perform some action. In this chapter we will look at two different kinds of causative verbs: one older (*rise-raise, sit-set, lie-lay*) and a more modern way of expressing causation (verb + object + infinitive).

Older causative verbs

The older set of causative verbs is a group of three pairs of verbs that drive both native and nonnative speakers crazy: *rise-raise, sit-set,* and *lie-lay*. To understand how the verbs in each of these pairs is related, we need to go back in time. At an earlier stage of English, there was a special ending that could be attached to an intransitive verb. (Reminder: Intransitive verbs have no objects, e.g., "The sun is shining." Transitive verbs must have objects, e.g., "I saw Bob last night.") The ending created a new transitive verb with the meaning of "to cause the action of the intransitive verb." For example, if the ending were attached to the verb *jump*, the new verb would mean "to cause someone to jump." If it were attached to the verb *sleep*, the new verb would mean "to cause someone to sleep." (Adding to the confusion, at a later stage of English, this causative ending produced a sound change in the transitive causative verbs so that the original intransitive verbs and the new transitive causative verbs no longer had the same vowels. This same vowel change is also responsible for many irregular nouns in English. For example: *man-men, tooth-teeth, mouse-mice*.)

Rise-raise

The intransitive verb *rise* means to "go up" or "get up." For example:

> The sun **rises** in the east.
> The curtain **has risen** and the play is about to begin.
> We **rose** at 4:30 this morning to catch the early flight.

As you would expect, the causative verb *raise* is a transitive verb that means "to cause someone or something to rise." (*Raise* in this meaning is virtually synonymous with *lift*.) For example:

> I **am raising** the window to let in a little air.
> They **raised** the curtain and the play began.
> If you have any questions, please **raise** your hand.

Over the years, the meaning of *raise* has broadened considerably. For example:

> She **raised** three children on her own. (*raise* = bring up)
> A lot of cotton **is raised** in California. (*raise* = grow)
> He **raises** money for nonprofit organizations. (*raise* = get)

The intransitive verb *rise* is irregular while the causative transitive verb *raise* is regular:

	INTRANSITIVE VERB *RISE*	TRANSITIVE CAUSAL VERB *RAISE*
Base/present tense	rise/rises	raise/raises
Past tense	rose	raised
Past participle	risen	raised
Present participle	rising	raising

EXERCISE
9·1

Use the correct form of rise *or* raise *in the blank. The first question is done as an example.*

Whenever a judge enters a courtroom, the court clerk says, "All _____*rise*_____."

1. The plantation owners in Virginia grew rich _____ tobacco.

2. Musicians who work late into the night never _____ before noon.

3. Our electricity rates have been _____ at about 20 percent a year.

4. Do you think you can _____ the money?

5. The captain _____ the anchor and the boat got under way.

6. I was born in Kansas, but _____ in California.

7. Congress has again voted to _____ the ceiling on the national debt.

8. A _____ tide lifts all boats.

9. Supposedly, women's skirt length _____ and falls according to the ups and downs of the stock market.

10. A lot of eyebrows were _____ when the congressman said that.

Sit-set

The intransitive verb *sit* means "to be seated" or "to be situated or placed." For example:

> Please **sit**.
> The students **were sitting** everywhere: on desks, on chairs, and on the windowsills.
> Their house **sits** on a hill overlooking the valley.
> The gallbladder **sits** on top of the liver.

Note that when we use *sit* in the second meaning of "to be situated or placed," *sit* must always be followed by an adverb of place. If this adverb is deleted, the sentence becomes ungrammatical. For example:

> X Their house **sits.**
> X The gallbladder **sits.**

The original meaning of the transitive verb *set* meant "to cause someone or something to sit or be placed somewhere." For example:

> He **set** all of his toy animals on top of the dresser.
> I **set** the vase of flowers on the table.
> A ladder **had been set** under the window.

Note that the transitive verb *set* requires not only an object but also an adverb of place.

In other words, when we set something we have to set it SOMEWHERE. If the adverb of place is deleted, the sentence becomes ungrammatical. For example:

> X He **set** all of his toy animals.
> X I **set** the vase of flowers.
> X A ladder **had been set.**

Over time, the original meaning of *set* has broadened to also mean "to arrange" or "to assign or pick." For example:

> I need to **set** the table before dinner.
> They **have** finally **set** the date for their wedding.

These other, newer meanings of *set* do not require an adverb of place to be grammatical.

Adding to the already substantial confusion of *sit* and *set* is the fact that *set* can be used as a noncausative, intransitive verb with the meaning of "to descend or go down." For example:

> The sun rises in the east and **sets** in the west.

This new use of *set* is sufficiently similar to the meaning and grammar of *sit* that it badly undercuts the historical distinction between *sit* and *set*. As a result, the two words have become confused with each other.

Another, much less confusing use of *set* as an intransitive verb also developed: the meaning of "to harden or become fixed." For example:

> The cement will **set** in about an hour.
> Their attitudes are completely **set** and inflexible.

The intransitive verb *sit* is irregular. The transitive causative verb *set* is also irregular, but in a special way. *Set* is one of these odd one-syllable verbs ending in a *t* or *d* that uses the same form for the present tense, the past tense, and both participles. This group of verbs is discussed in detail Chapter 7, "Talking about past time."

	INTRANSITIVE VERB *SIT*	TRANSITIVE CAUSAL VERB *SET*
Base/present tense	sit/sits	set/sets
Past tense	sat	set
Past participle	sat	set
Present participle	sitting	setting

Use the correct form of sit *or* set *in the blank. (Ignore the use of* set *meaning "to descend.") The first question is done as an example.*

We were all _____*sitting*_____ around the kitchen table when the lights went out.

1. Please _____ wherever you can find a seat.

2. I _____ my keys on the table in the hall so I can always find them.

3. No one wants to _____ next to the door because there is a terrible draft.

4. The dates have not been _____ in stone.

5. "I'm _____ on top of the world."

6. The fort _____ in a narrow valley where it commands the only road.

7. The waiter _____ the coffee on the table, spilling about half of it.

8. The judge came into the courtroom, his face _____ in an angry frown.

9. Everyone was _____ under a big oak tree where there was some shade.

10. Has the agenda been _____?

Lie-lay

This is the most difficult pair of causative verbs to use because of a historical accident: the past tense of the irregular intransitive verb *lie* happens to be *lay*, which is also the present-tense form of the regular transitive verb *lay*. For example:

> *Lie:*   An old dog **lay** on the porch. (past tense)
> *Lay:*   The dogs always **lay** their heads on my lap. (present tense)

Understandably, the similarity of these two forms has led to a lot of confusion about which verb is which.

The intransitive verb *lie* originally meant "to be in a horizontal position." For example:

I had to **lie** down for a moment.
The man **lay** facedown on the grass.
The book **lay** open on the table.

Over time this meaning has broadened to mean "to be placed." For example:

From the observation tower the entire city **lay** before us.
Their property **lies** to the north of us.

As we would expect, the transitive causative verb *lay* means "to cause to lie"—that is, "to place" or "to spread out." For example:

He **laid** his cards on the table.
The movers will **lay** the rugs for us.

Lay is also used metaphorically. For example:

They **laid** a trap for us.
They **laid** great stress on employees' being on time.

In casual conversation, there is a tendency to (incorrectly) use *lay* in place of *lie*. For example:

X He just **lays** around the house all day.

Needless to say, this use of *lay* is completely out of place in formal language.

If you have trouble with *lie* and *lay*, it might be worthwhile to memorize the following sentence:

We **lie** around, but we **lay** something down.

The intransitive verb *lie* is irregular. The transitive causative verb *lay* is regular.

	INTRANSITIVE VERB *LIE*	TRANSITIVE CAUSAL VERB *LAY*
Base/present tense	lie/lies	lay / lays
Past tense	lay	laid
Past participle	lain	laid
Present participle	lying	laying

Use the correct form of lie *or* lay *in the blank. The first question is done as an example.*

We ___*laid*___ tiles in the bathroom floor.

1. Just _____ back and enjoy the flight.

2. The old house had _____ in ruins for years.

3. She _____ her hand on the dog to calm him down.

4. The foundation for the church had been _____ around 1880.

5. Fortunately, his wallet was _____ right where he had left.

6. When the exam is over, everyone must _____ their pencils down.

7. The little town _____ deep in the valley.

8. The best _____ plans of mice and men often go astray.

9. He _____ back and closed his eyes.

10. We have been _____ around far too long.

More modern causative verbs

Modern English has a number of verbs that act as causatives. Most of these verbs require an object plus an infinitive. For example:

The storm **caused** <u>the roof on the barn</u> <u>to collapse.</u>
                              object   infinitive

I **asked** <u>the waiter</u> <u>to get us an outside table.</u>
                   object   infinitive

We **got** <u>the committee</u> <u>to change the next meeting date.</u>
                  object   infinitive

However, two of the more important causative verbs, *make* and *have*, do not take an infinitive. Instead these two verbs require a base-form verb (base-form verbs are sometimes called **bare infinitives**). For example:

I **made** <u>the kids</u> <u>clean up their rooms.</u>
      object   base form
We **had** <u>the contractor</u> <u>replace the leaking window in our bedroom.</u>
       object   base form

The fact that *make* and *have* take a base-form verb instead of the more common infinitives means that nonnative speakers often mistakenly use these two causative verbs with infinitives. For example:

X I **made** <u>the kids</u> <u>to clean up their rooms.</u>
       object   infinitive
X We **had** <u>the contractor</u> <u>to replace the leaking window in our bedroom.</u>
       object   infinitive

EXERCISE
9·4

Select the correct form by underlining either the infinitive or the base-form verb from the options inside the parentheses. The first question is done as an example.

The directions **require** us (<u>to reboot</u> / reboot) the computer.

1. We **asked** the people at the next table (to turn / turn) off their cell phones.

2. They **directed** us (to take / take) the left path back to the village.

3. The approaching deadline **made** all of us (to hurry / hurry) faster than was safe.

4. I always need to **remind** the children (to brush / brush) their teeth.

5. Please **have** him (to return / return) my call as soon as possible.

6. Everyone **wanted** Mary (to reject / reject) their offer.

7. **Make** them (to be / be) quiet!

8. The blinding light from the setting sun **forced** us (to pull / pull) off the road.

9. I **had** the gardener (to trim / trim) all of the hedges.

10. You **can't make** me (to do / do) it!

The passive

This chapter examines (1) how the *be* passive is formed, (2) the reasons for deleting the agent, and (3) the *get* passive.

How the *be* passive is formed

The passive is certainly the most complicated of all verb constructions in English. Chapter 5, "Verb forms and tenses," gives the basic rule that governs the formation of all the complex tense constructions in English. Complex constructions consist of two components: a specific helping verb followed by specific verb-tense form. The passive is no exception. In its most common form, the passive consists of these two components: some form of the helping verb *be* + a verb in the past participle form.

> The story **was read** by the whole class.
> *be* + past participle
> Lunch **will be provided**.
> *be* + past participle
> The money **had been kept** in a locked safe.
> *be* + past participle
> The children **are being watched** by a neighbor.
> *be* + past participle

Note that in the last example above there are two uses of the verb *be*: the first is for the progressive, the second is for the passive.

The signature of the passive is *be* (in some form) + a past participle. Any other use of *be* or of past participles does not constitute the passive. For example, the following sentence uses *be* as a helping verb, but it is not a passive because the *be* verb is not followed by a past participle:

> They **were eating** dinner when we got there.

The following sentence contains a past participle, but it is not a passive because the helping verb is not some form of *be*:

> They **had** already **eaten** dinner when we got there.

The following sentences contain a number of verb constructions in bold. If the verb construction is passive, write "passive" above the verb. If it is not passive, explain what element is missing. The first question is done as an example.

The players **had** finally **united** as a solid team.

be as a helping verb is missing

1. The kids **were** busy **helping** the neighbors pick tomatoes.

   _____

2. The initial proposal **had** originally **been met** with a lot of resistance.

   _____

3. The ghost of the lost hunter **has** never **appeared** again.

   _____

4. The presentation **will be continued** after lunch.

   _____

5. They **have** apparently **learned** nothing from their experience.

   _____

6. The dogs **should have been taken** to the vet this afternoon.

   _____

7. We **are making** them a very attractive offer.

   _____

8. Some of the paperwork **must have been lost** along the way.

   _____

9. Many students **are carrying** far too many credits.

   _____

10. His story **will** never **be believed.**

    _____

Passives are unique in that they are actually derived from another construction. Thus there is a special paraphrase relationship between every passive sentence and its active counterpart. Sentences that are in the passive are said to be in the **passive voice**. Sentences that are not passive are said to be in the **active voice** (a term that is rarely used except in discussing the passive). Every passive sentence has been derived from a corresponding active sentence by a special set of rules. Here is an example:

> *Active*   Anne **wrote** the final report of the committee.
> *Passive*   The final report of the committee **was written** by Anne.

There are three changes from the active sentence to its passive paraphrase, which we can imagine taking place in the following three-step process:

1. The original subject of the active sentence *(Anne)* is turned into the object of a *by* prepositional phrase and moved to the end of the sentence.

2. The original object of the active sentence (*the final report of the committee*) moves forward to fill the now empty subject slot.

3. The helping verb *be* is inserted in front of the main verb in whatever tense the original main verb was in, and the main verb is changed into a past participle. In this example, the verb *be* is used in the past tense *was* and the main verb is used in the past participle form *written*.

The tense of the active sentence is always retained in the passive paraphrase. If the active is in the present tense, the passive must also be in the present tense. If the active is in the past tense, the passive must also be in the past tense. For example, in the following example, the tense of the original active sentence is kept in the passive paraphrase:

> *Active*   Anne always <u>**writes**</u> the final report of the committee.
>   present tense
> *Passive*   The final report of the committee <u>**is**</u> always <u>**written**</u> by Anne.

The passive verb must agree with the new subject, not the original one. For example, if the above example had the original object in the plural, the passive would change to plural to agree with the new subject:

> The final reports of the committee **are** always written by Anne.
>   present tense   past participle

If the active sentence has one or more helping verbs, the *be* of the passive is inserted right in front of the main verb (always the right-most verb). The form of the inserted *be* always takes on the tense form of the original main verb. (The main verb, of course, has to change to the past participle form.)

Here are some more examples of this process.

The active contains a modal verb:

> *Active*   We **should mail** the letter as soon as possible.
>   ‾‾‾‾‾‾‾ ‾‾‾‾
>   past tense base form
>
> *Passive*   The letter **should be mailed** as soon as possible.
>   ‾‾‾‾‾ ‾‾ ‾‾‾‾‾
>   past   base   past
>   tense form   participle

The active contains a perfect tense:

> *Active*   Someone **had written** a letter of complaint.
>   ‾‾‾ ‾‾‾‾‾‾
>   past tense past participle
>
> *Passive*   A letter of complaint **had been written** by someone.
>   ‾‾‾ ‾‾‾‾ ‾‾‾‾‾‾
>   past   past   past
>   tense part   part

The active contains a progressive tense:

> *Active*   The engineers **were testing** the machine.
>   ‾‾‾‾ ‾‾‾‾‾‾
>   past tense present part
>
> *Passive*   The machines **were being tested** by the engineers.
>   ‾‾‾‾ ‾‾‾‾‾ ‾‾‾‾‾‾
>   past   pres   past
>   tense part   part

EXERCISE 10·2

Change the following active sentences into their passive equivalents. Label all the verb forms in the passive sentences. The first question has been done as an example.

We **had** already **paid** the phone bill.
  ‾‾‾   ‾‾‾‾
  past   past part

The phone bill had already been paid .
‾‾‾‾‾‾‾‾‾‾‾‾‾‾‾‾‾‾‾‾‾‾‾‾‾‾‾‾‾‾‾‾‾
         past   past   past
                         part   part

1. They **will require** an answer immediately.

   pres base form

   _____

2. The kids **are choosing** a new pet.

   pres pres
         part

   _____

3. They **have entered** the data in the wrong column.

   pres past part

   _____

4. The police **should have investigated** the accident.

   past   base   past
           form   part

   _____

5. They **have made** a new offer.

   pres past
         part

   _____

6. They **are losing** too much time.

   pres past
         part

   _____

7. They **could have postponed** the meeting.

   past base   past
         form   part

   _____

8. I **will** not **be using** the car tomorrow.

   pres   base   pres
          form   past

   _____

9. Their lawyers **might** **have** **filed** a new motion.
      past base past
             form part

10. They **should** **have** **taken** the train.
     past   base   past
             form part

How does the passive paraphrase differ from the original active form? There is no real difference in meaning: the new passive sentence still means the same thing as the original active sentence. What has changed is the focus. The passive paraphrase shifts the focus of attention away from the doer of the action (the original subject) to what was done (the original object). For example, let's look again at our original example of active and passive sentences:

> *Active*   Anne **wrote** the final report of the committee.
> *Passive*   The final report of the committee **was written** by Anne.

The active sentence focuses on what Anne did. The passive sentence focuses on the final report of the committee. One problem in talking about the meaning of active and passive sentences is that the term **subject** is confusing. Anne is the grammatical subject of the active sentence but not of the passive sentence. The grammatical subject of the passive sentence is the noun phrase *the final report of the committee* even though Anne is still the semantic subject of the sentence, that is, the doer of the action.

Reasons for deleting the agent

We need to introduce a term that may be new to you: **agent**. The agent always plays the role of doer of the action of the sentence. In an active sentence, the grammatical subject is also the agent. But in a passive sentence, the grammatical subject is not the agent.

Since the whole point of using the passive is to shift focus away from the agent and focus instead on what was done, why do we even want to keep the agent in the passive sentence? The answer is that most of the time we do not keep the agent. Studies of written English have shown that the agent is deleted from passive sentences about 85 percent of the time.

The main reason the agent is deleted is that the agent is usually one of the following: (1) unknown or unknowable, (2) an impersonal entity or institution, (3) universal or highly generalized, or (4) embarrassing or awkward to reveal. Here are some examples:

1. unknown or unknowable agent:

> My bike **was stolen** last night.
> Most diamonds **are mined** in Africa.

2. impersonal entity or institution:

> Our flight **was** just **canceled**.
> She **was promoted** to regional manager recently.

3. universal or highly generalized agent:

> World War I **has been** largely **forgotten.**
> Mass transit **should be** more widely **used.**

4. agent withheld because embarrassing or awkward:

> Mistakes **were made**.
> We **were given** some bad advice.

EXERCISE

10·3

All of the following sentences are passives whose agents have been deleted. Select which of the following four options best characterizes the reason for dropping the agent: (1) unknown or unknowable agent, (2) impersonal entity or institution, (3) universal or highly generalized agent, or (4) agent withheld because embarrassing or awkward. The first question is done as an example.

Passives **should be avoided**.

_____(3) universal or highly generalized agent_____

1. New guidelines **have been issued**.

_____

2. My new cell phone **was made** in China.

_____

3. Your son **has been sent** to the principal's office.

_____

4. The word *judgment* **is** often **misspelled**.

_____

5. The walls **had been covered** in graffiti.

_____

6. We **were** always **told** not to talk to strangers.

_____

7. I'm sorry, but your credit card application **has been rejected**.

_____

8. Thrift **is** more often **praised** than practiced.

_____

9. The airport **has been closed**.

_____

10. The movie **was filmed** on location in Paris.

_____

One of the most common pieces of advice given to professional or technical writers is to avoid the passive unless there is a compelling reason to use it. Often the passive, especially in any kind of formal writing, is overused, making the writing pompous and lifeless—like the worst kind of bureaucratic writing. Good writers use the passive form of a sentence when there is a reason for it. A common reason for using the passive is to focus on and expand the object portion of the underlying active sentence rather than the agent. For example, see how Thomas Jefferson used the passive in the following excerpt from the Declaration of Independence, one of the most important documents in American history:

> We hold these truths to be self-evident, that all men **are created** equal, that they **are endowed** by their Creator with certain unalienable Rights.

Jefferson could have used the active rather than the passive:

> We hold these truths to be self-evident, that the Creator **created** all men equal, that He **endowed** them with certain unalienable Rights.

Clearly, Jefferson wanted *all men* to be the focus of the sentence rather than the agent *the Creator*. He thus shifted the sentence into its passive form.

A good writing practice is to test a passive against its active form to see which one works best. Unless there is a good reason to prefer the passive, we should consider rephrasing the sentence in its active form. To do this, we need to be able to consciously convert a passive to its active form. Here is an example:

> *Passive*   The proposal **was rejected** by a slim majority.

Whether the active or passive is more appropriate depends entirely on the context and what the writer's intentions are. But consciously looking at both forms ensures that we will not use an inappropriate passive just because we did not consider the alternative active form.

Creating the active form is a two-step process:

1. Switch the two noun phrases: move the agent into the subject position and move the subject of the passive to an object position (deleting the preposition *by*).

2. Change the form of the main verb to whatever tense the helping verb *be* is in and then delete the *be*.

Here is how we might convert the passive example above into its underlying active structure:

> *Passive*   The proposal **was rejected** by a slim majority.

1. Switch noun phrases and delete *by*:

> The proposal **was rejected** by a slim majority. ⇒
> A slim majority **was rejected** the proposal

2. Change the main verb to the same tense as *be* and then delete *be*:

> A slim majority **was rejected** the proposal ⇒
> A slim majority **rejected** the proposal

Here is a second example with a more complicated verb:

> *Passive*   The boat **might have been stranded** by the low tide.

1. Switch noun phrases and delete *by*:

> The boat **might have been stranded** by the low tide. ⇒
> The low tide **might have been stranded** the boat.

2. Change the main verb to the same tense as *be* and then delete *be*:

The low tide **might have been stranded** the boat. ⇒
The low tide **might have stranded** the boat.

Note that none of the verbs in front of the passive helping verb *be* is affected by the change to the active.

EXERCISE
10·4

Convert the following passive sentences to their active form. The first question is done as an example.

Our lost kitten **was** soon **returned** by some neighbors.

   Some neighbors soon returned our lost kitten.

1. Several alternative treatments **were offered** by the doctor.

   _____

2. The tomatoes **had been grown** in our garden by the children.

   _____

3. The oath of office **was being administered** by the Chief Justice.

   _____

4. A valuable lesson **had been learned** by everyone.

   _____

5. The police **should have been alerted** by the people in the neighborhood.

   _____

6. The tumor **was** first **identified** by an MRI scan.

   _____

7. The company **was being bought out** by a large corporation.

   _____

8. The accident **would have been covered** by the local paper.

   _____

9. Fortunately, the crew **was rescued** by the Coast Guard.

_____

10. The door **had been forced open** by someone during the night.

_____

Get passives

There is a second form of passive voice that uses *get* rather than *be* as the passive helping verb. The basic rule for the passive that the helping verb must be followed by a past participle still holds. Here are some examples with both the *get* passive and the *be* passive:

get passive:	The cats **got fed** this morning.
be passive:	The cats **were fed** this morning.
get passive:	They lost because they **got outsmarted**.
be passive:	They lost because they **were outsmarted**.
get passive:	Theo **got selected** for the program.
be passive:	Theo **was selected** for the program.

Even though *get* is used as a passive helping verb, *get* cannot be used to form questions and negatives in the same way that *be* can. For example:

get passive:	The cats **got fed** this morning.
Question:	**Did** the cats **get fed** this morning?
Negative:	The cats **didn't get fed** this morning.
be passive:	The cats **were fed** this morning.
Question:	**Were** the cats **fed** this morning?
Negative:	The cats **weren't fed** this morning.

The difference between the *be* passive and the *get* passive is that *be* is a helping verb that can form questions and negatives without any additional verb. However, *get* is not a helping verb so it requires the addition of the helping verb *be* to form questions and negatives.

While the *get* and *be* passives are interchangeable in some cases, there are many cases in which they cannot be interchanged. The biggest difference is in degree of formality. *Get* passives are primarily used in casual, spoken language and are rarely used in formal writing. For example, it would be unimaginable to find this in a book or article:

X Abraham Lincoln **got assassinated** in 1865.

Instead, we would find the *be* passive:

Abraham Lincoln **was assassinated** in 1865.

Get passives have idiosyncratic uses and restrictions, probably a result of their highly colloquial, even slangy nature. For example, a study of *get* passives found that 95 percent of the time, the passive was used without the agent *by* phrase.

Get passives are most likely to be used with dynamic verbs, verbs that have a strong sense of action or decisive activity. For example:

He **got injured** playing football.
I **got caught** in a traffic jam on the way to work.
She **got assigned** to a new project.

Get passives are not used much with nondynamic verbs, verbs that do not express action. If they are used with nondynamic verbs, the resulting passives are often ungrammatical. For example:

X John **hasn't gotten** seen for weeks.
X The accident **got photographed** right after it happened.
X The noise **got heard** everywhere in the building.

The same sentences are completely grammatical if the *be* passive is used instead of the *get* passive:

John **wasn't seen** for weeks.
The accident **was photographed** right after it happened.
The noise **was heard** everywhere in the building.

EXERCISE
10·5

Each of the following sentences contains a be *passive in bold. Replace the* be *passive with the corresponding* get *passive UNLESS the* get *passive is used with a nondynamic verb. In that case, write "ungrammatical." The first two questions are done as examples.*

We all **were** badly **bitten** by mosquitoes.

We all got badly bitten by mosquitoes.

The party **was enjoyed** by everyone.

ungrammatical

1. I **was selected** to give the introduction.

   _____

2. Last year's mistakes **were avoided** this year.

   _____

3. All of us **were sunburned** on our camping trip.

   _____

4. They **were pulled** out of the ditch by a tow truck.

   _____

5. They **were permitted** to park on the lawn this year.

   _____

6. **Were** all of the items **sold**?

   _____

7. Their efforts **were** greatly **appreciated**.

   _____

8. **Wasn't** their e-mail **answered**?

   _____

9. **Was** she **hurt** in the accident?

   _____

10. The queen **was** not **amused**.

   _____

The structure of adjective clauses

11

In this chapter we will examine how adjective clauses are constructed. In particular, we will examine (1) the internal structure of adjective clauses, (2) creating and moving relative pronouns, (3) deleting relative pronouns, and (4) moving objects of prepositions.

Adjective clauses function in two different ways depending on whether or not they restrict the meaning of the nouns they modify. This distinction between **restrictive** and **nonrestrictive adjective clauses** is discussed in detail in the next chapter. In this chapter, however, we will ignore the distinction between restrictive and nonrestrictive clauses because both types are constructed the same way. All of the examples in this chapter will be of restrictive adjective clauses.

The internal structure of adjective clauses

Adjective causes have a distinct internal structure: they must begin with a **relative pronoun**. For this reason, adjective clauses are often called **relative clauses.** In the following examples, the adjective clauses are underlined and the relative pronouns are in bold.

> I need the book **that** is on the shelf behind you.
> The young man **who** answered the door is her cousin.

Relative pronouns have no independent meaning of their own, but instead take their meaning from the nouns in the main sentence that the adjective clauses modify. These nouns are called the **antecedents** of the relative pronouns. In the first example, the antecedent of *that* is *book*. In the second example, the antecedent of *who* is *man*.

Normally adjective clauses immediate follow their antecedents. Sometimes, though, antecedents can be followed by short modifiers that separate them from the relative pronouns that begin the adjective clauses. For example:

> I met a man at work **who** says he knows you.

113

Obviously the antecedent of *who* is *man*, not the nearest noun *work*. Separating adjective clauses from their antecedents is legitimate as long as they are still close together and it is perfectly clear which noun is the antecedent of the relative pronoun.

There are several different relative pronouns. Which pronoun we use is determined by the nature of the antecedent. The following chart summarizes the relative pronouns that go with each type of antecedent:

ANTECEDENT	RELATIVE PRONOUN
Human	*who, whom, whose* (see note)
Nonhuman	*that* (we will ignore *which* for the moment)
Spatial noun	*where*
Temporal noun	*when*

Note: In conversation, *that* is used to refer to human antecedents about 30 to 40 percent of the time. We will ignore this informal usage in this presentation.

Here is an example of each type of antecedent:

Human	I like teachers **who** stick to their lesson plans.
Nonhuman	Did you get the e-mail **that** I sent you?
Spatial noun	I left my glasses in the room **where** we met this afternoon.
Temporal noun	It was a period **when** the whole world was at war.

EXERCISE

11·1

In the following sentences, the adjective clauses have been underlined, but the spaces for the relative pronouns have been left blank. Determine which relative pronoun should be used and write it in the blank space. In this exercise we will only use who *for human antecedents (i.e., you won't need* whom *and* whose*). The first question is done as an example.*

Take the first right turn ( ) you come to.

Take the first right turn (that) you come to.

1. Use the desk ( ) is next to the window for now.

_____

2. I finally got the mosquito ( ) had bothered me all night.

_____

3. We searched for a place ( ) we could cross the river.

_____

4. I wanted you to meet the people ( ) were so helpful during the power outage.

_____

5. Let's pick a time ( ) we can all meet.

_____

6. I can't stand the sugary cereal ( ) the kids eat.

_____

7. I only know the people in the building ( ) work in finance.

_____

8. My parents live in a little town ( ) everyone knows everyone else.

_____

9. The symptoms ( ) I had were pretty typical.

_____

10. It was a period ( ) everything seemed to go wrong all at once.

_____

Relative pronouns are the link between the adjective clause and the noun in the main sentence that the adjective clause modifies (the relative pronoun's antecedent). As we have seen, the antecedent determines both the meaning of the relative pronoun and which relative pronoun is used.

However, INSIDE the adjective clause, the relative pronoun plays a normal pronoun role that has nothing to do anything outside the adjective clause. Inside its adjective clause, the relative pronoun is like any other pronoun: it can be the subject of its clause; it can be an object of the verb; it can be the object of a preposition; or it can be a possessive pronoun that modifies a noun. It can also be used in an adverbial prepositional phrase where it expresses spatial or temporal meaning. Here are some examples with both human and nonhuman pronouns. The relative pronoun is in bold and the entire adjective clause is underlined.

Subject	He is a friend **who** is always willing to help.
	We finally found the key **that** unlocks the old cedar chest.
Object	He is a friend **whom** I have known for years.
	We finally found the key **that** I thought I had lost.
Object of Preposition	The singer **whom** we told you about is going to be on TV tonight.
	We bought the first house **that** we looked at.
Possessive	He is a person **whose** word no one would doubt.
Nonhuman antecedents	The bus **whose** wheel fell off was on the side of the road.
Spatial	We found a hotel **where** we could all stay.
Temporal	It was a time **when** their business was just getting started.

EXERCISE
11·2

Identify which of the following six roles the relative pronouns play in the adjective clauses below: **subject, object, object of preposition, possessive, spatial,** *or* **temporal.** *The first question is done as an example.*

We located the person **whose** truck had been blocking our driveway.

    Possessive

1. I didn't know the person **whom** they were discussing.

   _____

2. We talked to some of the other parents **whose** children go to the same school as ours.

   _____

3. Some of the tests **that** were done earlier need to be redone.

   _____

4. We went to a restaurant **where** they serve Middle Eastern food.

   _____

5. The farmhouse **that** my grandparents used to live in was finally torn down last year.

   _____

6. We were able to refinance the mortgage **that** we have on our house.

   _____

7. I couldn't remember the name of the person **who** first told me that.

   _____

8. Find someone **whose** cell phone can get a signal.

   _____

9. The mall **that** we went to is way over on the other side of town.

   _____

10. I had to return the CD **that** I just bought because it was defective.

    _____

Creating and moving relative pronouns

One of the distinctive characteristics of adjective clauses is that they begin with relative pronouns. When the relative pronoun plays the role of subject in its own clause, the relative pronoun is automatically at the beginning of the adjective clause. But how do all the other nonsubject relative pronouns get to the beginning of the adjective clause? Answer: we must move all nonsubject relative pronouns to the beginning of the adjective clause. We will now look at this complex process in more detail.

All adjective clauses start out as statements that use the antecedent noun in some role within the adjective clause. (The antecedent must be in the underlying adjective clause or else the adjective clause would not be a statement about the antecedent.)

In all the examples below, we will put the underlying adjective clause in parentheses to remind us that this underlying clause must be converted to an actual relative clause. The repeated antecedent noun is in bold.

The process of converting the underlying adjective clause to an actual adjective clause takes two steps:

1. Replace the antecedent with the appropriate relative pronoun.

2. Move the relative pronoun to the first position in the adjective clause.

The first step has to factor in two totally independent pieces of information: first, the nature of the antecedent noun itself (i.e., we have to decide whether the antecedent noun is

human, nonhuman, spatial, or **temporal**), and second, the role of the antecedent noun inside the adjective clause (i.e., we have to decide whether the antecedent noun is acting as **the object of a verb, the object of a preposition, a possessive noun, a spatial noun,** or **a temporal noun**). These two pieces of information are represented in the following table:

	OBJ OF VERB	OBJ OF PREP	POSSESSIVE	SPATIAL	TEMPORAL
Human	whom	whom	whose		
Nonhuman	that	that			
Spacial				where	
Temporal					when

The second step is to move the relative pronoun to the first position inside the adjective clause. Here is an example that uses a nonhuman antecedent noun as the object of the verb:

Underlying sentence   They own some property (they want to sell **the property**).

The first step is to replace the antecedent noun with the appropriate relative pronoun:

that

They own some property (they want to sell ~~the property~~).

The second step is to move the relative pronoun to the first position inside the adjective clause:

They own some property **that** they want to sell.

Here is a second example, but this time the antecedent noun is human:

I met the teacher (you liked **the teacher** so much).

whom

Step 1   I met the teacher (you liked ~~the teacher~~ so much).
Step 2   I met the teacher **whom** you liked so much.

Here are examples of antecedent nouns playing each of the remaining roles:

Object of a preposition

I got the iPod (I was telling you about **the iPod**).

that

Step 1   I got the iPod (I was telling you about ~~the iPod~~).
Step 2   I got the iPod **that** I was telling you about.

Possessive

I called up the man (I found **the man's dog**).

whose

Step 1 I called up the man (I found ~~the man's~~ dog).
Step 2 I called up the man <u>whose dog</u> I found.

Notice that when we move a possessive pronoun, we must also move the noun that the possessive modifies. In the example above, "whose dog" moves as a single unit.

Spatial

I know the building (he works **in the building**).

where

Step 1 I know the building (he works ~~in the building~~).
Step 2 I know the building <u>where he works</u>.

Temporal

Six P.M. was the time (we had agreed to meet **at the time**).

when

Step 1 Six P.M. was the time (we had agreed to meet ~~at the time~~).
Step 2 Six P.M. was the time <u>when we had agreed to meet</u>.

Note: The adverbial relative pronouns *where* and *when* replace the entire adverbial prepositional phrase.

EXERCISE
11·3

Use the two-step process to form an adjective clause from the underlying sentences. The first question is done as an example.

We took the road (the guide book recommended **the road**).

We took the road ___*that the guide book recommended*___ .

1. We learned that from the students (we met **the students** on the campus tour).

_____

2. The police were searching the area (the campers had last been seen **in that area**).

_____

3. I remember the day (she was born **on the day**).

_____

4. He is a person (one could always turn to **the person**).

_____

5. I will introduce you to the teacher (you will be taking **the teacher's** class).

_____

6. Two thousand three was the year (they were married **in that year**).

_____

7. Do you know the place (they are planning to meet **in the place**)?

_____

8. Unfortunately, he is a man (no one can depend on **the man**).

_____

9. She is the author (we are reading **the author's** book in my literature class).

_____

10. They visited Sutter's Mill (gold was first discovered in California **at Sutter's Mill**).

_____

Deleting relative pronouns

Two roles that antecedent nouns play inside relative clauses have more than one way of being realized as relative clauses: the objects of verbs and the objects of prepositions. By far the most important of these are antecedent nouns that play the role of objects of verbs. For relative pronouns that do NOT play the role of subject, there is a third optional step: delete the relative pronoun. Here are two examples, one with a human noun and one with a non-human noun:

I called the people (they had selected **the people**).

	whom
Step 1	I called the people (they had selected ~~the people~~).
Step 2	I called the people **whom** they had selected.
	∅
Step 3 (optional)	I called the people ~~whom~~ they had selected.

Note: We will use the null symbol ∅ to represent an element that has been deleted from the sentence.

We saw the movie (you recommended **the movie**).

	that
Step 1	We saw the movie (you recommended ~~the movie~~).
Step 2	We saw the movie **that** you recommended.
	∅
Step 3 (optional)	We saw the movie ~~that~~ you recommended.

Here are some more examples of deleted relative pronouns playing nonsubject roles:

Object of a preposition
The issue ~~that~~ they had been arguing about has been resolved.

Spatial
Do you know a place ~~where~~ we can get a cup of coffee?

Temporal
I can remember a time ~~when~~ we would have stayed up late for it.

We cannot delete possessive relatives because we would be left with an ungrammatical fragment of a noun phrase:

∅
X I called up the man ~~whose dog~~ I found.

This option of deleting nonsubject relative pronouns is commonly used. In fact, in conversation, the relative pronoun is omitted about 25 percent of the time according to a major study.

When the relative pronoun is deleted from the beginning of an adjective clause, the truncated relative clause is much more difficult to recognize for the obvious reason that the relative pronoun, the flag word that normally signals the beginning of the relative clause, is no longer there.

All of the following sentences contain an unidentified adjective clause with a deleted relative pronoun. Underline the adjective clause and confirm your answer by restoring the appropriate relative pronoun at the beginning of the adjective clause. The first question is done as an example.

I answered the only question I got.

I answered the only question that I got.

1. We really like the color you painted the living room.

_____

_____

2. The children we saw must belong to the couple next door.

_____

_____

3. The time we were supposed to meet will not work after all.

_____

_____

4. The food they serve in the cafeteria would choke a goat.

_____

_____

5. Everyone hopes that the place we want to meet is still available.

_____

_____

6. We talked to the young couple you told us about.

_____

_____

7. The defense challenged the evidence the prosecution presented at the trial.

_____

_____

8. They were happy to accept the offer we had agreed on.

_____

_____

9. The dean congratulated the seniors the department chairs had nominated.

_____

_____

10. We ended up buying the place the real estate agent had taken us.

_____

_____

Moving objects of prepositions

The second area in which there is an option in how relative pronouns are treated is when antecedent nouns play the role of object of a preposition. Let us take as an example the following underlying sentence:

> We met the new senator (so much has been written about **the new senator**).

Step 1 is the same:

> whom
> We met the new senator (so much has been written about ~~the new senator~~).

Step 2 has an option. We can move the relative pronoun to the first position of the adjective clause as we have done before, producing

> We met the new senator **whom** so much has been written about.

Or we can move BOTH the pronoun AND the preposition that controls the pronoun, producing this alternative form of the adjective clause:

> We met the new senator **about whom** so much has been written.

Both of these alternatives are fully grammatical. However, there is substantial difference between practices in spoken language and formal written language. When we are speaking (except for the most formal, almost ceremonial occasions) we would move the relative pronoun by itself. In formal written language, many writers would move both the preposition and the relative pronoun. This choice reflects a traditional (if somewhat old-fashioned) reluctance to end sentences with prepositions.

With nonhuman antecedents the alternative of moving the preposition is a little more complicated because we have to use the relative pronoun *which* in step 1 instead of the usual relative pronoun *that*. For example:

We rented the movie (we heard so much about **the movie**).

Step 1   We rented the movie (we heard so much about **the movie**).
                                                                        which
Step 2   We rented the movie **about which** we heard so much.

If we move the preposition, we no longer have the option of deleting the relative pronoun:

$$\varnothing$$
X We rented the movie about **which** we heard so much.

EXERCISE
11·5

Turn the following underlying sentences into two different forms of adjective clauses, the first where the relative pronoun has moved by itself and the second where the relative pronoun and the preposition move together. The first question is done as an example.

The new conductor (we just learned about **the new conductor**) is from Germany.

The new conductor ___*whom we just learned about*___ is from Germany.

The new conductor ___*about whom we just learned*___ is from Germany.

1. The gate (we had driven earlier through **the gate**) was closed by the police.

_____

_____

2. The story (we reported on **the story** last night) has become national news.

_____

_____

3. The people (we made friends with **the people**) invited us over for dinner.

_____

_____

4. We made an offer on the apartment (we looked at **the apartment** yesterday).

_____

_____

5. We finally resolved the issues (we had been fighting about **the issues** for some time).

_____

_____

6. We had to reconsider the items (we had not budgeted for **the items**).

_____

_____

7. He was finally given the reward (he was entitled to **the reward**).

_____

_____

8. I brought up the issues (we had talked about **the issues** before).

_____

_____

9. We went back to the doctor (we had previously consulted with **the doctor**).

_____

_____

10. We bought the house (my parents had lived in **the house**).

_____

_____

Restrictive and nonrestrictive adjective clauses

This chapter deals with two topics: (1) the differences in meaning between restrictive and nonrestrictive adjective clauses, and (2) the reduction of adjective clauses to participial phrases.

The differences in meaning between restrictive and nonrestrictive adjective clauses

Adjective clauses play two very different roles. One role, called **restrictive**, significantly affects the meaning of the noun it modifies by limiting or narrowing the meaning of that noun. (All of the examples that we examined in the previous chapter, "The structure of adjective clauses," were restrictive.) Here is a clear-cut example of a restrictive adjective clause (underlined):

All students <u>who fail the final exam</u> will fail the course.

The restrictive adjective clause *who fail the final exam* significantly narrows the meaning of *student* from all students to a specific subclass of students, namely, those students who fail the final exam. If we delete the restrictive adjective clause, it completely changes the meaning of the original sentence:

All students will fail the course.

Nonrestrictive adjective clauses, on the other hand, give additional information about the nouns they modify, but this information does not affect or alter the basic meaning of that noun. Typically, nonrestrictive adjective clauses give supplementary information. For example:

>My parents, <u>who live in a little town</u>, enjoy visiting us in New York.

The nonrestrictive adjective clause *who live in a little town* does not define or limit who the speaker's parents are. They would still be the speaker's parents even if they did not live in a little town. If we delete the nonrestrictive adjective clause, the deletion does not change the basic meaning of the noun *parents*.

>My parents enjoy visiting us in New York.

Obviously, the meaning contained in the nonrestrictive adjective clause is lost if we delete the clause. In this example, the information in the nonrestrictive clause gives an implied reason why the speaker's parents enjoy visiting New York—they are from a small town and thus especially enjoy the things that can only be found in a large metropolitan area. However, the scope of the meaning of the noun phrase *my parents* is not changed by the deletion.

It is a mistake to think of the information in nonrestrictive clauses as being unimportant information. Sometimes it is quite important. The key distinction between restrictive and nonrestrictive clauses is the effect of the information on the nouns that they modify. If the information significantly alters or narrows the meaning of the noun it modifies, then the modifier is restrictive. If it does NOT significantly alter or narrow the meaning, then the modifier is nonrestrictive.

The distinction between restrictive and nonrestrictive adjective clauses is signaled in both speech and writing. In speech, restrictive and nonrestrictive adjective clauses have noticeably different phrasal groupings and intonation patterns.

Restrictive adjective clauses are pronounced in the same phrase unit with the nouns they modify. There is a distinct pause between the end of the restrictive adjective clause and the rest of the sentence. For example:

>All students <u>who fail the final exam</u> | will fail the course.
>(The symbol | indicates the boundary of a phrase unit.)

The entire unit consisting of the antecedent noun and the restrictive adjective clause phrase is said with a steady upward intonation that drops abruptly in pitch at the end of the restrictive adjective clause. In our example, the drop in pitch is after *exam* and before *will*.

Nonrestrictive adjective clauses are cut off by pauses at both the beginning and the end of the nonrestrictive clause. For example:

My parents | who live in a little town | enjoy visiting us in New York.

The entire nonrestrictive adjective clause is also said at a lower pitch level than the rest of the sentence. For example:

My parents | | enjoy visiting us in New York.
          who live in a little town

In the written language, the difference between restrictive and nonrestrictive adjective clauses is marked by a difference in punctuation. Restrictive clauses are NEVER set off with commas, while nonrestrictive clauses are ALWAYS set off with commas. For example:

Restrictive	The airplane that we flew in was an Airbus.
Nonrestrictive	Newark, which is actually in New Jersey, is New York's busiest airport.

Here are some observations that may help you decide whether an adjective clause is restrictive or nonrestrictive.

Virtually all adjective clauses that modify proper nouns are nonrestrictive. Proper nouns name a unique individual, place, or thing. Therefore any modifying adjective does not provide defining information, only supplementary information.

Most restrictive adjective clauses define which person, place, or thing is being talked about. For example:

I need the names that you collected.

The adjective clause *that you collected* tells us which names the speaker is talking about. Without this information, we would have no idea which names the speaker means.

The best way to tell if an adjective clause is restrictive or not is to delete the adjective clause from the sentence and see if it changes the basic meaning of the sentence. If it does, the adjective clause is restrictive. If it does not, it is nonrestrictive.

Write "Rest" if the clause is restrictive and "Nonrest" if it is nonrestrictive. Then supply commas if the clause is nonrestrictive. The first question is done as an example.

The Sydney Opera House <u>which is right on the harbor</u> is world famous.

__*Nonrest*__ The Sydney Opera House, __*which is right on the harbor*__ ,

is world famous.

1. _____ My car <u>which is fifteen years old</u> has never needed a major repair.

2. _____ The car <u>that is in front of us</u> is leaking oil badly.

3. _____ You should call your father <u>who seemed very anxious to talk to you.</u>

4. _____ I just bumped into my high school math teacher <u>whom I hadn't seen in years.</u>

5. _____ The math teacher <u>who taught me algebra in the ninth grade</u> did a really good job.

6. _____ The Congo River <u>which crosses the equator twice</u> flows both north and south.

7. _____ There is only one man in town <u>who can repair foreign cars.</u>

8. _____ The people <u>whom we met at lunch</u> seemed very nice.

9. _____ The town <u>where they live</u> is about fifty miles from Seattle.

10. _____ A police officer <u>who seemed to come out of nowhere</u> stopped all the traffic.

There are two differences between restrictive and nonrestrictive adjective clauses: (1) the use of *that* and *which*, and (2) the deletion of relative pronouns playing the role of objects of verbs in restrictive and nonrestrictive clauses. To see the differences, compare the following sentences.

Restrictive	I bought a book **that** <u>you recommended.</u>
Nonrestrictive	I got out my Blackberry, **which** <u>I had just bought that morning.</u>

In formal writing, *that* is reserved for restrictive adjective clauses and *which* for nonrestrictive. Sometimes in less formal writing and often in conversation, *that* and *which* are both used in restrictive clauses, for example:

Restrictive	I bought a book **that** you recommended.
Restrictive	I bought a book **which** you recommended.

However, even in the most casual conversation *that* cannot be used in nonrestrictive clauses:

Nonrestrictive	X I got out my Blackberry, **that** I had just bought that morning.

As was discussed in the previous chapter, relative pronouns that are used as objects of verbs can optionally be deleted, for example:

Restrictive	I bought a book **that** you recommended.
Restrictive	I bought a book ∅ **that** you recommended.

The option to delete an object relative pronoun is limited to restrictive adjective clauses. If we try to delete an object relative pronoun from a nonrestrictive clause, the result is ungrammatical. For example:

Nonrestrictive	I got out my Blackberry, **which** I had just bought that morning.
Nonrestrictive	X I got out my Blackberry, ∅ ~~which~~ I had just bought that morning.

EXERCISE 12·2

***That, which,* or ∅?** *The adjective clauses in the following sentences are underlined. Above the word* Relative, *use* that, which, *or* ∅ *if the relative pronoun replaces the object of a verb. If the adjective is nonrestrictive, add commas as appropriate. The first question is done as an example.*

∅
I beat the record **Relative** I had set the year before.

1. The first layer of paint **Relative** was a white undercoat dried in less than an hour.

2. The snowstorm **Relative** we had been worrying about turned out to be nothing.

3. He called a meeting **Relative** is in conflict with an important client session.

4. The mouse came out of a hole **Relative** I had never even noticed before.

5. My workday **Relative** was pretty long to begin with was extended thirty minutes.

6. His temperature **Relative** had now climbed to 103 degrees was beginning to scare us.

7. We need to rent a truck **Relative** is big enough to hold all this stuff.

8. During the concert, my cell phone **Relative** I had forgotten to turn off rang loudly.

9. He swatted hopelessly at a mosquito **Relative** was buzzing around our heads.

10. The only menus **Relative** the restaurant had were in Italian.

The reduction of adjective clauses to participial phrases

Adjective clauses of a certain type can be reduced to what are called **participial phrases**. Participial phrases contain either a **present participle** or a **past participle.** Here are some examples of participial phrases with the whole participial phrase underlined and the participle itself in bold:

Present participial phrase

We got a hotel room **facing** the beach.
The teacher, **looking** at the clock, brought the lesson to a close.

Past participial phrase

He always has pancakes **smothered** in maple syrup.
The team, **unbeaten** in its last ten games, made it to the playoffs.

Notice that some of the above examples of participial phrases are surrounded by commas and some are not. The ones with commas are restrictive participial phrases; the ones without commas are nonrestrictive participial phrases. When adjective clauses are reduced to participial phrases, the participial phrase inherits the restrictive or nonrestrictive status of its parent adjective phrase.

There is a very strict rule that governs which adjective clauses can be reduced and which cannot. To be reduced to a participial phrase, the adjective clause must contain the helping verb *be* (in some form) followed by either a present participle or a past participle.

The *be* + present participle sequence comes from a verb in the progressive tense. The *be* + past participle sequence comes from a verb in the passive.

Let us now compare the original relative clauses that were the source of the four participial phrase examples above:

Present participial phrase

Clause   We got a hotel room <u>that **was facing** the beach</u>.
Phrase   We got a hotel room **facing** the beach.

Clause   The teacher, <u>who **was looking** at the clock</u>, brought the lesson to a close.
Phrase   The teacher, **looking** at the clock, brought the lesson to a close.

Past participial phrase

Clause   He always has pancakes <u>that **are smothered** in maple syrup</u>.
Phrase   He always has pancakes **smothered** in maple syrup.

Clause   The team, <u>which **was unbeaten** in its last ten games</u>, made it to the playoffs.
Clause   The team, **unbeaten** in its last ten games, made it to the playoffs.

To reduce an adjective clause to a participial phrase, we delete the relative pronoun and the helping verb *be*. For example:

Clause   The man <u>who is standing next to her</u> is her cousin.
Phrase   The man ~~who is~~ <u>standing next to her</u> is her cousin.

Clause   His book, <u>which is based on his life</u>, has become a bestseller.
Phrase   His book, ~~which is~~ <u>based on his life</u>, has become a bestseller.

EXERCISE
12·3

Underline the adjective clauses in the following sentences and reduce the adjective clauses to participial phrases. The first question is done as an example.

He always likes french fries <u>~~that are~~ smothered in ketchup</u>.

1. The course, which is required for all new employees, is offered every month.

2. The books that are required for the course may be purchased at the office.

3. Drivers who are renewing their licenses after January 1 must take an eye exam.

4. We talked to the reporter who was covering the story.

5. All of the children who were born after 2004 have been vaccinated.

6. He is always looking for stocks that are selling at historically low prices.

7. The company, which was once nearly destroyed by labor disputes, is now doing well.

8. The mechanic found the problem that was causing the car to suddenly lose power.

9. Sunlight that was reflected off the building was blinding drivers on the highway.

10. Her first book, which was published when she was only twenty, became a bestseller.

Some present participial phrases are probably not formed directly from reduced adjective clauses because the verb that is the source of the participle cannot be used in the progressive. For example:

Clause	X The driver, who **was seeing** the accident, put the brakes on.

The verb *see* is a stative verb, and stative verbs cannot be used in the progressive tenses. (See Chapter 6, "Talking about present time," for a discussion of stative verbs.) However, present participial phrases with stative verbs are perfectly grammatical:

Phrase	The driver, **seeing** the accident, put the brakes on.

Presumably at some time in the past, people began using stative verbs in participial phrases in imitation of regular participial phrases formed from reduced adjective clauses.

Nonrestrictive participial phrases of all kinds have a unique property: they can be moved away from the nouns they modify. (No other noun modifier of any kind can do this.) For example, compare the following pairs of participial phrases, the first in its normal position following the noun it modifies and then the same participial phrase shifted.

Normal	The wave, swelling high over our heads, crashed against the boat.
Shifted	Swelling high over our heads, the wave crashed against the boat.
Normal	My parents, exhausted by the grandkids, went to bed early.
Shifted	Exhausted by the grandkids, my parents went to bed early.
Shifted	My parents went to bed early, exhausted by the grandkids.

Typically, participles modifying the subject are the ones that are moved. Usually, the participial phrase is shifted to the beginning of the sentence, but as you can see in the second example above, sometimes the participial phrase can be shifted to the far end of the sentence.

Restrictive participial phrases cannot be shifted. For example:

Normal	Statements <u>made by the defendant</u> were entered into evidence.
Shifted	X <u>Made by the defendant</u>, statements were entered into evidence.

Participial phrases modifying personal pronouns are often shifted. For example:

Normal	He, <u>being a vegetarian</u>, often has trouble ordering at restaurants.
Shifted	<u>Being a vegetarian</u>, he often has trouble ordering at restaurants.

When the pronoun is a first-person pronoun, shifting the participial phrase is virtually mandatory. For example:

Normal	We, <u>having lost our lease</u>, began looking for a new apartment.
Shifted	<u>Having lost our lease</u>, we began looking for a new apartment.

EXERCISE
12·4

Underline the participial phrases in the following sentences. If the participial phrase is nonrestrictive, move it to an appropriate place. Be sure to add the necessary commas. The first question is done as an example.

My parents hearing the good news called to congratulate us.

My parents, <u>hearing the good news</u>, called to congratulate us.

<u>Hearing the good news, my parents called to congratulate us.</u>

1. The new apple developed to be pest-resistant has proved a commercial success.

   _____

2. Many college students living on their own for the first time incur far too much

   debt. _____

3. She rushing to answer the phone slipped on the rug and fell. _____

   _____

4. Someone walking past the house noticed the smoke. _____

   _____

5. I having no background in the matter whatsoever stayed out of the debate. _____

   _____

6. Children just beginning to walk cannot be left alone for a minute. _____

_____

7. The man stopping dead in his tracks stared at us in amazement. _____

_____

8. A person involved in the dispute cannot offer an impartial opinion. _____

_____

9. We presented with such an unusual opportunity decided to act at once. _____

_____

10. The police acting on an anonymous tip arrested the gang leader. _____

_____

Gerunds

13

In this chapter we will examine two aspects of using gerunds: (1) identifying gerunds, and (2) determining the expressed and unexpressed subjects of gerunds.

Identifying gerunds

A gerund is the *-ing* (present participle) form of a verb used as an abstract noun. For example, look at the following sentence:

> **Complaining** doesn't do any good.

The gerund *complaining* is used as a noun that plays the role of the subject of the sentence.

Since gerunds are derived from base-form verbs, gerunds are often used with the complements (such as objects) and adverbs that often accompany the base-form verb. For example, in the following sentence

> <u>**Answering** the phone all day long</u> is not a very exciting job.

The gerund *answering* is used along with the base-form verb's object *the phone* and the adverbial expression *all day long*. Technically, the term **gerund** is reserved for just the *-ing* verb form while the gerund together with its complements and adverbs is called a **gerund phrase**. Since gerunds and gerund phrases act exactly alike, we will use **gerunds** as a collective term for both gerunds and gerund phrases unless there is a specific reason to distinguish between a gerund and a gerund phrase. In all example sentences, the gerund will be in bold and the entire gerund phrase will be underlined (as in the example immediately above).

Gerunds can be used in all three of the common noun roles of subject, object, and object of a preposition. (We will discuss the fourth, less common, noun role of predicate nominative later.) For example:

Subject	**Answering** my e-mails takes all morning.
	Losing a close game is always hard.
Object	I love **eating** out at nice restaurants.
	My job often requires **working** weekends and holidays.
Object of a preposition	I took care of **fixing** dinner.
	We should ask about **getting** an extension.

Gerunds cannot be used in all noun positions. The basic rule is that gerunds can be used only where we can also use **abstract nouns**. Abstract nouns refer to intangible concepts—as opposed to animate and concrete nouns that refer to living things and objects, respectively. Some useful abstract nouns are *effort, success, idea, problem,* and *outcome.* It is a good bet that wherever you can use one or more of these abstract nouns, you can also use a gerund. For example, see how all the gerunds above are used in places where abstract nouns could also be used:

Subject

Answering my e-mails takes all morning.
   The effort

Losing a close game is always hard.
     Success

Object

I love **eating** out a nice restaurants.
       The idea

My job often requires **working** weekends and holidays.
         The effort

Object of a preposition

I took care of **fixing** dinner.
    The problem

We should ask about **getting** an extension.
     The problem

Noun positions that require animate or concrete nouns will not allow gerunds. For example, the verb *jump over* requires an animate subject:

_____ jumped over the fence and ran away.

None of our test abstract nouns can be used as subjects with this verb:

X **The effort** jumped over the fence and ran away.
X **Success** jumped over the fence and ran away.
X **The idea** jumped over the fence and ran away.
X **The problem** jumped over the fence and ran away.
X **The outcome** jumped over the fence and ran away.

As we would expect, it is impossible to use gerunds as subjects of the verb *jump over*:

X **Answering** my e-mails jumped over the fence and ran away.
X **Losing** a close game jumped over the fence and ran away.

The verb *crash* requires a concrete subject:

_____ crashed to the ground.

None of our test abstract nouns can be used as subjects of *crash*:

X **The effort** crashed to the ground.
X **Success** crashed to the ground.
X **The idea** crashed to the ground.
X **The problem** crashed to the ground.
X **The outcome** crashed to the ground.

Accordingly, we cannot use gerunds as subjects of the verb *crash*:

X **Answering** my e-mails crashed to the ground.
X **Losing** a close game crashed to the ground.

Each of the following sentences has a blank space where a noun belongs. Use the test abstract nouns effort, success, problem, idea, *or* outcome *to determine whether or not gerunds could be used in that noun space. If the abstract nouns do not make sense, write "no gerund." If they do make sense, write "gerund" and confirm your answer by writing an appropriate gerund in the space. The first question is done as an example.*

_____ made us rethink what we were doing.

Gerund The outcome made us rethink what we were doing.

Getting such poor results made us rethink what we were doing.

1. _____ proved that we were capable of doing the job.

_____

_____

2. _____ wished that we had more time.

_____

_____

3. They need to encourage _____.

_____

_____

4. I am very worried about _____.

_____

_____

5. John offered to drive _____ to the airport.

_____

_____

6. Can you explain _____?

_____

_____

7. We fully support _____.

_____

_____

8. I argued against _____.

_____

_____

9. The kids ate _____ for breakfast this morning.

_____

_____

10. The media dismissed _____ as unimportant.

_____

_____

The first step in learning how to use gerunds is knowing how to identify them. Fortunately, there is a simple and completely reliable test to tell when an -*ing* verb form is being used as a noun: replace the gerund phrase (or gerund if it is used by itself) with the pronoun *it*. Using the *it* pronoun test works because gerunds are always singular. Also, we don't have to worry about subject or object forms because *it* can be used in either role. The *it* substitution test is also extremely helpful in that it exactly defines the boundary of the entire gerund phrase. Here is the *it* pronoun replacement test used with the example sentences above:

Subject
Answering <u>my e-mails</u> takes all morning.
      It

Losing <u>a close game</u> is always hard.
      It

Object
I love **eating** <u>out a nice restaurants.</u>
        it

My job often requires **working** <u>weekends and holidays.</u>
          it

Object of a preposition

Before **painting** the room, we need to move all the furniture.
                 it

We should ask about **getting** an extension.
                                  it

EXERCISE

13·2

Underline the gerunds in the following sentences. (Note: There may be more than one gerund.) Confirm your answer by using the it *substitution test. The first question is done as an example.*

I will try <u>working from home</u>.
                   it

1. Finishing my thesis on time required some real sacrifices.

   _____

2. You need to think about taking some time off.

   _____

3. I really enjoy working in my garden.

   _____

4. He insisted on paying the bill.

   _____

5. They are not happy about having to attend a seven o'clock meeting.

   _____

6. Enjoying one's work is the key to job satisfaction.

   _____

7. I couldn't stand taking all those statistics classes.

   _____

8. He felt a lot better after taking a nap.

   _____

9. Taking Latin is really good for improving one's vocabulary.

_____

10. Getting the early flight will avoid getting stuck in traffic.

_____

Gerunds can also be used for predicate nominatives. **Predicate nominatives** are nouns that follow linking verbs and are used to describe or rename the subject. For example:

> Joan is **an economist**.

Joan = an economist.

> His book became **a bestseller**.

His book = a bestseller.

> Their new office building resembles **a minimum-security prison**.

Their new office building = a minimum-security prison.

Here are some examples of gerunds used as predicate nominatives:

> The biggest problem is **getting** the job finished on time.

The biggest problem = getting the job finished on time.

> The difficulty is **acquiring** an adequate staff.

The difficulty = acquiring an adequate staff.

> My own worry is **commuting** such a great distance every day.

My own worry = commuting such a great distance every day.

Identifying gerunds used as predicate nominatives is very hard to do because the sequence of _be_ + _-ing_ verb form looks just like the progressive tense. For example, look at the following sentence:

> John is talking on the telephone.

Here the sequence of _be_ + _-ing_ verb form is a present-tense progressive, not a gerund used as a predicate nominative. How on earth can we tell such similar-looking forms apart?

There are two reliable tests. The positive test for gerunds is, of course, the *it* substitution test. For example:

The biggest problem is **getting** the job finished on time.
                        it

The difficulty is **acquiring** an adequate staff.
                   it

My own worry is **commuting** such a great distance every day.
                 it

When we try to apply the *it* substitution test to a progressive, the result is nonsensical. For example,

John is talking on the telephone.
        X it

Talking on the telephone is not a noun phrase. Therefore, *talking on the telephone* does not rename *John* or describe who *John* is:

X John = talking on the telephone

The positive test for deciding if the sequence *be* + *-ing* verb form is a progressive tense is to see if you can replace the progressive tense with the past tense. For example:

John is talking on the telephone.
Past-tense test   John talked on the telephone.

Since the substitution of the past tense makes perfect sense, we have positive proof that the sequence of *is* + *talking* is the progressive form of the verb *talk*.

Whenever we see the sequence of *be* + *-ing* verb form, there are two possible grammatical interpretations:

1. **Progressive.** *be* is a helping verb followed by a main verb in an *-ing* or present participle form.

2. **Gerund.** *be* is the main verb followed by a gerund functioning as a predicate nominative.

To see how helpful these two tests are, compare the following sentences that appear identical except for the subject:

John is watching sports on TV.
His main activity is watching sports on TV.

The two sentences look completely parallel, but they are actually totally different.

Sentence 1 is a present progressive as we can show by using the past-tense test:

> John is <u>watching</u> sports on TV.
> John <u>watched</u> sports on TV.

When we try this same test on sentence 2, the result is nonsensical:

> His main activity is <u>watching</u> sports on TV.
> X His main activity <u>watched</u> sports on TV.

Sentence 2 is a gerund as we can show by using the *it* substitution test to show that what follows the verb *be* is a noun phrase, and since the noun phrase follows the linking verb *be*, it can only be a predicate nominative that renames the subject:

> His main activity is <u>watching sports on TV.</u>
>   it
>
> his main activity = watching sports on TV

Determine whether the underlined sequences in the following sentences are gerunds or part of progressives. Confirm your answer by using the it *and the past-tense substitution tests and an equals statement. The first question is done as an example.*

My job is <u>editing tech support documents</u>.

Answer: gerund

It substitution test: My job is <u>editing tech support documents</u>.
                                                            it

Past-tense sub test: X My job edited tech support documents.

Equals statement: My job = editing tech support documents.

1. Every CEO's dream is <u>beating performance expectations</u>.

    Answer: _____

    It substitution test: _____

    Past-tense sub test: _____

    Equals statement: _____

2. My English assignment is <u>summarizing a chapter of the book</u>.

   Answer: _____

   It substitution test: _____

   Past-tense sub test: _____

   Equals statement: _____

3. A concern of every city in the Southwest is <u>getting enough water</u>.

   Answer: _____

   It substitution test: _____

   Past-tense sub test: _____

   Equals statement: _____

4. John is <u>getting pretty good at playing tennis</u>.

   Answer: _____

   It substitution test: _____

   Past-tense sub test: _____

   Equals statement: _____

5. My problem is <u>remembering everything I am supposed to do</u>.

   Answer: _____

   It substitution test: _____

   Past-tense sub test: _____

   Equals statement: _____

6. Most American companies are <u>providing adequate health insurance</u>.

   Answer: _____

   It substitution test: _____

   Past-tense sub test: _____

   Equals statement: _____

7. Their great concern is <u>providing adequate health insurance</u>.

Answer: _____

It substitution test: _____

Past-tense sub test: _____

Equals statement: _____

8. A coach's responsibility is <u>getting the athletes in good condition</u>.

Answer: _____

It substitution test: _____

Past-tense sub test: _____

Equals statement: _____

9. A big part of an office manager's job is <u>ordering supplies</u>.

Answer: _____

It substitution test: _____

Past-tense sub test: _____

Equals statement: _____

10. Our office manager is <u>thinking about getting new computers</u>.

Answer: _____

It substitution test: _____

Past-tense sub test: _____

Equals statement: _____

Determining the expressed and unexpressed subjects of gerunds

We saw in the previous section that gerunds are derived directly from verbs. Gerunds carry over many aspects of their underlying source verb. For example, we saw that gerund phrases preserve the complements and adverbs from their base-form verb sources.

The verbs underlying gerunds also have subjects—just as other verbs do. All of the gerunds that we have examined so far have not retained their underlying subjects. We will now refer to these kinds of gerunds as gerunds with **unexpressed subjects**. Gerunds that have retained their underlying subjects will be called gerunds with **expressed subjects**. Here are examples of each type:

Unexpressed subject	**Missing** too many meetings makes a bad impression.
Expressed subject	Larry's **missing** the meeting got him into trouble.

The unique feature of expressed subjects is that they MUST be in the possessive form. To see how gerunds with expressed subjects are derived, we will use the same convention as we did in Chapter 11, "The structure of adjective clauses," and put the underlying sentence in parentheses. Here is how we would convert the underlying sentence:

We argued about (Robert **changed** the deadline)

into an actual gerund phrase. The first step is to change the tensed verb (the past tense *changed* in this example) into an *-ing* form, creating the gerund *changing*:

changing
Step 1   We argued about (Robert ~~changed~~ the deadline)

If we were not preserving the subject of the gerund, we would delete *Robert* to produce the final sentence with an unexpressed subject:

We argued about **changing** the deadline.

This is how all the gerunds in this chapter have been produced up to now.

When we preserve the subject from the sentence underlying the gerund, we do so by changing the subject noun phrase into a possessive noun phrase. In this example, we will change the subject noun *Robert* into the possessive noun *Robert's*:

Robert's
Step 2   We argued about (~~Robert~~ **changing** the deadline).

The final form of the sentence is the following:

We argued about Robert's **changing** the deadline.

Here is a second example, this time with the entire gerund phrase playing the role of subject of the verb in the main sentence. In this example the subject of the gerund is a pronoun:

(We got badly lost) caused us to miss the flight.

getting
Step 1 (We **got** badly lost) caused us to miss the flight.

Our
Step 2 (~~We~~ **getting** badly lost) caused us to miss the flight.
Our **getting** badly lost caused us to miss the flight.

Each of the following sentences contains a sentence in parentheses. Reduce this sentence to a gerund phrase, retaining the subject as a possessive. Use the same two-step process illustrated above. The first question is done as an example.

The fans were worried about (the team lost its star player).

Step 1: The fans were worried about (the team losing its star player).

Step 2: The fans were worried about the team's losing its star player.

1. (The bank approves the loan) made it possible for us to go ahead.

   Step 1: _____

   Step 2: _____

2. Everyone resented (he unfairly criticized the school board).

   Step 1: _____

   Step 2: _____

3. We were delayed by (the children needed to take an afternoon nap).

   Step 1: _____

   Step 2: _____

4. (The defendant told a convincing story) persuaded the jury that he was innocent.

   Step 1: _____

   Step 2: _____

5. What made her so successful was (she was such a good listener).

Step 1: _____

Step 2: _____

6. Try to ignore (they behaved so rudely).

Step 1: _____

Step 2: _____

7. The odds against (he wins the election) were pretty big.

Step 1: _____

Step 2: _____

8. The campers barely survived (they got lost in the woods).

Step 1: _____

Step 2: _____

9. (I became sick) nearly spoiled our vacation.

Step 1: _____

Step 2: _____

10. We all have to get used to (our children grow up and leave home).

Step 1: _____

Step 2: _____

Clearly, when the subject of the gerund is expressed, we know who performed the action of the gerund. The real question, though, is how do we interpret the subject of the gerund when it is unexpressed? Sometimes there is no way to tell the subject of a gerund except from context or some previous knowledge.

Many times, however, our interpretation of unexpressed subjects is guided by a set of default interpretations. There is no guarantee that these interpretations are correct; nevertheless, these are the interpretations that listeners and readers will place on the unexpressed subjects in the absence of any other information. There are two sets of default interpretations, one for when gerunds are used as subjects of their sentences and a second set for when gerunds are used as objects of verbs or objects of prepositions.

When gerunds are used as subjects, there are two likely default interpretations of their unexpressed subjects. One is that we look for a plausible noun following the main verb that we can use as the unexpressed subject of the gerund. Here are some examples:

<u>**Missing** that phone call</u> caused **Susan** a lot of problems later.

Susan is the default unexpressed subject of *missing*.

<u>**Smiling** at the customers</u> doesn't cost **you** anything.

You is the default unexpressed subject of *smiling*.

The next example is a bit more complicated:

<u>**Getting** two cavities</u> caused the dentist to give **me** a real scolding.

There are two noun phrases that follow the main verb. *Dentist*, the first noun phrase, does not make sense as the unexpressed subject of *getting*. The dentist did not scold me because the dentist got two cavities. The dentist scolded me because the speaker (*me*) got two cavities.

If there is no noun phrase following the main verb that could possibly function as the subject of the gerund, a likely default interpretation is that the gerund is being used to make a generalization. For example:

<u>**Missing** too many meetings</u> makes a bad impression.

We would all interpret this gerund as a generalization about what happens to people who miss too many meetings.

Here are some more examples of subjectless gerunds used to make generalizations:

<u>**Playing** a musical instrument</u> takes a big commitment.
<u>Instinctively **knowing** what to do in a crisis</u> is the mark of a natural leader.

Underline the gerunds used as subjects in the following sentences. Determine whether the gerund is used to make a generalization or whether some noun phrase after the verb can serve as the unexpressed subject of the gerund. If it is a generalization, write "generalization." If the latter case is true, identify which noun phrase it is. The first question is done as an example.

<u>Breaking a small bone</u> in his foot caused the team's star player to miss three games.
the team's star player is the unexpressed subject of the gerund.

1. Getting it right the first time is the main goal.

   _____

2. Running twenty miles a week really helped Sam lose weight.

   _____

3. Complaining about the weather all the time is pointless.

   _____

4. Talking to Bob about his children's bad behavior only makes him angry at us.

   _____

5. Having to commute hours each way is really hard on a family.

   _____

6. Trying to please everybody got her into a lot of trouble.

   _____

7. Going back to school for a master's degree is one of George's options.

   _____

8. Training one's replacement is something that all good administrators should do.

   _____

9. Improving her GPA was Julie's main reason for going to summer school.

   _____

10. Publishing papers is a major part of being a university professor these days.

   _____

When gerunds are used as objects of verbs or objects of prepositions (particularly when there is no other noun phrase between the main verb and the gerund), the most common default interpretation of unexpressed subjects is that the subject of the sentence is also the unexpressed subject of the gerund. For example:

Objects of verbs	Jack tried **starting** <u>the car again.</u>
	Jack is the person starting the car.
	The car barely **avoided** <u>sliding into the ditch.</u>
	The car is what almost slid into the ditch.
Objects of prepositions	My parents talked about **going** <u>to</u> <u>Hawaii for their anniversary.</u>
	My parents are going to Hawaii.
	We looked into **refinancing** <u>the mortgage on our house.</u>
	We are the ones considering refinancing the mortgage.

EXERCISE
13·6

Each of the following sentences contains a sentence in parentheses that functions as the object of a verb or preposition. Reduce this sentence to a gerund phrase. If the subject of the gerund is identical to the subject of the main verb, delete the subject, creating an unexpressed subject. If the subject of the gerund is different from the subject of the main verb, retain the subject in the appropriate possessive form. The first two questions are done as examples.

The workers debated about (the workers go on strike).

The workers debated about ____*going on strike*____ .

I can't accept his argument for (the company closes the plant).

I can't accept his argument for ____*the company's closing the plant*____ .

1. I deeply regretted (I went back on my promise to them).

_____

2. The ad promoted (families choose a healthier diet).

_____

3. Her family was pleased with (Mary got her degree).

_____

4. I concentrated on (I kept just the right tension on the kite string).

_____

5. We approved of (he ordered pizza for the kids).

_____

6. I asked my advisor about (I go to business school next year).

_____

7. We certainly appreciated (we got such good service).

_____

8. The kids sensed (we began to get worried about the storm).

_____

9. Everyone predicted (our team won the championship).

_____

10. The canoe race totally depended on (the river had enough water).

_____

Infinitives

14

In this chapter we will examine two aspects of using infinitives: (1) identifying infinitives, and (2) determining the expressed and unexpressed subjects of infinitives.

Identifying infinitives

An **infinitive** consists of *to* + the base (or dictionary entry) form of a verb. For example:

to be	to go
to have	to sing

Since infinitives are derived from underlying verbs, we often use the underlying verb's complements or modifiers along with the infinitive form of the verb. When an infinitive is used with a complement or modifiers, the entire infinitive construction is called an **infinitive phrase**. Here are some examples of infinitives and infinitive phrases used as objects of verbs:

Infinitive	I need <u>to rest</u>.
Infinitive phrase	I need <u>to rest for a little while</u>.
Infinitive	We want <u>to go</u>.
Infinitive phrase	We want <u>to go home early tonight</u>.

The distinction between an infinitive and an infinitive phrase is rarely important or even helpful. Accordingly, we will use the plural term **infinitives** as a neutral term for both the simple infinitive and the expanded construction with complements and modifiers. We will use the technical terms **infinitive** and **infinitive phrase** only when this distinction is necessary for the discussion.

Infinitives resemble gerunds in many ways. However, there are several important differences. One big difference is that gerunds can only be used as nouns, but infinitives can be used as four different parts of speech: nouns, verb complements, adjectives, and adverbs modifying adjectives.

Here are some examples of each type. Note that the first example in each pair is an infinitive and the second example is an infinitive phrase.

Nouns	"To err is human . . ." (Alexander Pope)
	Our goal is to increase sales by 50 percent this year.
Verb complements	He asked us to leave.
	They agreed to cooperate on the project.
Adjectives	He is the man to see.
	The time to act on this urgent matter is now.
Adverbs modifying adjectives	Are you ready to go?
	We will be glad to see them again.

This section will concentrate only on infinitives used as nouns. This immediately raises the following question: how can we tell infinitives used as nouns from infinitives used as any of the three other parts of speech? The answer is that we will use the same test that we used in the previous chapter to identify gerunds: the *it* pronoun test. Only infinitives used as nouns can be replaced by the pronoun *it*. None of the infinitives used as other parts of speech can be replaced by *it*. The *it* test works so well because infinitives are always singular, and they always function as abstract nouns—features that are completely compatible with the characteristics of the pronoun *it*. Here is the *it* pronoun test applied to all of the examples given above that illustrate the four different ways that infinitives can be used. The *it* test only works with infinitives used as nouns.

Nouns	"To err is human . . ." (Alexander Pope)
	It
	Our goal is to increase sales by 50 percent this year.
	it
Verb complements	He asked us to leave.
	X it
	They agreed to cooperate on the project.
	X it
Adjectives	He is the man to see.
	X it
	The time to act on this urgent matter is now.
	X it
Adverbs modifying adjectives	Are you ready to go?
	X it
	We will be glad to see them again.
	X it

The infinitives in the following sentences have been underlined. Use the it *test to determine which of these infinitives is functioning as a noun. If the infinitive is a noun, write "noun" below the infinitive phrase. If it is not a noun, write "not a noun" below the infinitive phrase. The first question is done as an example.*

We always aim <u>to please our customers.</u>

It test: We always aim it <u>to please our customers.</u>

not a noun

1. The angry citizens demanded <u>to talk to the mayor.</u>

   _____

2. CNN just announced her <u>to be the winner.</u>

   _____

3. We are pleased <u>to welcome our distinguished visitors.</u>

   _____

4. <u>To really learn English grammar</u> takes a lot of time.

   _____

5. There seems <u>to have been a mistake.</u>

   _____

6. We will be sad <u>to leave such a nice place.</u>

   _____

7. The storm caused the river <u>to flood over its banks.</u>

   _____

8. We decided <u>to take her parents out to dinner.</u>

   _____

9. I am not prepared <u>to answer your questions at this time.</u>

   _____

10. Our original idea was <u>to stay home and order some Chinese food.</u>

   _____

Infinitives play the expected noun roles of subject, object of verb, and predicate nominative. For example:

Subject	To do your best is all anyone can ask of you.
	To turn down such a good opportunity doesn't make any sense.
Object of verb	I need to get a new printer as soon as I can.
	We tried to call you last night, but nobody was home.
Predicate nominative	My job is to review the language of all funding proposals.
	The final decision was to go with the in-house candidate.

Conspicuously absent from this list of noun roles is the role of object of a preposition. Infinitives, unlike gerunds, cannot be used as objects of prepositions. For example:

Infinitive	X We talked about to go out to lunch Friday.
Gerund	We talked about going out to lunch Friday.

The difference is striking. The infinitive phrase is totally unacceptable while the gerund phrase is completely acceptable. The reason infinitives cannot be used as the objects of prepositions is historical. The *to* that we use in infinitives is actually the preposition *to*. The *to* blocks the infinitive from being the object of the preceding preposition—prepositions cannot be the objects of other prepositions.

EXERCISE
14·2

Underline all of the infinitives in the following sentences. Use the it *test to determine which infinitives are used as nouns. If the infinitive is not a noun, write "not a noun" below it. If the infinitive is a noun, write its grammatical role (**subject, object of verb,** or **predicate nominative**) below it. The first question is done as an example.*

My main concern was to find a hotel that wouldn't wreck my budget.

ANSWER   My main concern was <u>to find a hotel that wouldn't wreck my budget.</u>

     it predicate nominative
     _____

1. To drive a heavy truck requires a special driver's license.

     _____

2. I really wanted to believe that everything would work out OK.

     _____

3. Our first class assignment was to determine how much a small company was worth.

_____

4. I decided to take the calculus course after all.

_____

5. To teach in middle school requires a person who really likes kids.

_____

6. I don't want to give up so easily.

_____

7. To get a new car would be more than we could afford right now.

_____

8. I am not ready to go to bed yet.

_____

9. Our main concern is to keep our costs down as much as humanly possible.

_____

10. We need to get ready to go.

_____

Determining the expressed and unexpressed subjects of infinitives

Infinitives, like gerunds, have subjects. All of the infinitives we have examined so far have not retained their underlying subjects. We will refer to these kinds of infinitives as having **unexpressed subjects**. Infinitives that retain their underlying subjects will be called infinitives with **expressed subjects**. Here are examples of each type:

Unexpressed subject	<u>To give up so easily</u> would be a sign of weakness.
Expressed subject	<u>For them to give up so easily</u> would be a sign of weakness.

The unique feature of expressed subjects is that they must be in a prepositional phrase beginning with the preposition *for*. Since the underlying subject is used as the object of the preposition *for*, we have the odd situation that pronouns that play the role of subject of the infinitive must be in the object form. This is the case of our example sentence above. We cannot keep the subject pronoun in its subject form:

> X For **they** to give up so easily would be a sign of weakness.

We must put the subject of the infinitive in an object form:

> For **them** to give up so easily would be a sign of weakness.

To see how infinitives with expressed subjects are derived, we will use the same convention as we did in the previous chapter on gerunds and put the underlying sentence in parentheses. Here is how we would convert the underlying sentence:

> I would like (she is our spokesperson at the meeting).

The first step is to change the tensed verb in the underlying sentence to an infinitive:

> **to be**
> *Step 1*   I would like (she **is** our spokesperson at the meeting).

If we were not preserving the subject of the infinitive, we would delete the underlying subject *she* to produce the final sentence with an unexpressed subject:

> I would like to be our spokesperson at the meeting.

This is how all the infinitives in this chapter have been produced up to now. However, as you can see, that sentence has a different meaning from what we are trying to express.

To preserve the subject from the sentence underlying the infinitive, we change the subject noun phrase into the object of the preposition *for*. In this example, we will change the underlying subject *she* into the prepositional phrase *for her*:

> **for her**
> *Step 2*   I would like (she to be our spokesperson at the meeting.)

The final form of the sentence is the following:

> I would like for her to be the spokesperson at the meeting.

Here is a second example, this time with the infinitive phrase playing the role of subject of the main verb in the sentence:

(I take charge of the committee) would be bit awkward

to take
Step 1 (I **take** charge of the committee) would be bit awkward.

For me
Step 2 (~~I~~ to take charge of the committee) would be a bit awkward.
Final form <u>For me to take charge of the committee</u> would be a bit awkward.

Even if the subject of the underlying sentence is a possessive noun phrase, the possessive noun phrase becomes the object of the preposition *for*. For example:

I contracted (John's band plays at our party)

to play
Step 1 I contracted (John's band **plays** at our party)

for John's band
Step 2 I contracted (~~John's band~~ to play at our party)
Final form I contracted <u>for John's band to play at our party</u>.

EXERCISE
14·3

Each of the following sentences contains a sentence in parentheses. Reduce this sentence to an infinitive phrase, retaining the subject as the object of the preposition for. *Use the same two-step process that is illustrated above. The first question is done as an example.*

We arranged (they meet each other).

Step 1   We arranged (they to meet each other).

Step 2   We arranged for them to meet each other.

1. Our final option was (the contractor replaces the entire front porch).

_____

_____

2. We would prefer (the children attend the after-school program).

_____

_____

3. (The company ignores state regulations) was a serious error.

_____

_____

4. John would hate (my friends are disappointed).

_____

_____

5. Our greatest fear would be (the pipes in our house froze while we were away).

_____

_____

6. (They take charge like that) really helped us a lot.

_____

_____

7. Most parents intend (their children inherit the parents' estate).

_____

_____

8. The plan was (we flew directly back after the conference was over).

_____

_____

9. (They got so upset over what happened) made everyone uncomfortable.

_____

_____

10. The farmers were all praying (the rain came in time to save the crops).

_____

_____

We have seen many examples of infinitives being used as subjects of sentences. Often English speakers prefer to move or transpose these subject infinitives to the end of the sentence. This is especially true if the infinitive phrase is long or complicated. We fill the now vacant subject position with a "dummy" or "empty" *it* to act as a subject placeholder. Here are some examples of transposed or shifted subject infinitives:

Original	To operate heavy equipment requires a special license.
Shifted	**It** requires a special license to operate heavy equipment.
Original	For me to work from home made a lot of sense.
Shifted	**It** made a lot of sense for me to work from home.
Original	For us to relocate to New York would cost a lot of money.
Shifted	**It** would cost a lot of money for us to relocate to New York.

If the main verb in the sentence is a linking verb followed by a **predicate adjective**, we nearly always transpose the subject infinitive. For example:

Original	To drive on the left side of the road seemed very strange.
	linking verb predicate adj
Shifted	**It** seemed very strange to drive on the left side of the road.

Here is another example:

Original	For them to get so upset over nothing seemed crazy.
Shifted	**It** seemed crazy for them to get so upset over nothing.

EXERCISE
14·4

Underline the infinitives used as subjects. Transpose the infinitives to the end of the sentence and put it *in the vacated subject position. The first question is done as an example.*

Not to get the promotion was a bit of a disappointment.

It was a bit of a disappointment not to get the promotion.

1. For us to accept the offer made perfect economic sense.

_____

_____

2. For them not to finish the job on time would be very costly.

_____

_____

3. For us to get an independent assessment of the costs seemed only prudent.

_____

_____

4. To have a very low voter turnout was Senator Blather's only hope.

_____

_____

5. For the whole family to go skiing at a resort would cost an arm and a leg.

_____

_____

6. To keep the house clean with children and pets takes a lot of work.

_____

_____

7. For him to say such a thing struck us as very strange.

_____

_____

8. For our company to go so deeply into debt worried everyone.

_____

_____

9. To contest the mayor's decision in court would take a lot of time and effort.

_____

_____

10. For us to lose the first two games would put us in an impossible position.

_____

_____

_____

The real problem is when the subject of the infinitive is unexpressed. When there is no expressed subject, our interpretation of the infinitive is guided by a set of default interpretations. There is no guarantee that these interpretations are correct; nevertheless, these are the interpretations that listeners and readers will place on the unexpressed subjects in the absence of any other information. There are two sets of default interpretations, one for when infinitives are used as the subjects of their sentences and a second set for when infinitives are used as objects of verbs.

When the infinitive plays the role of subject, there are two default interpretations of the missing subject. One is that we look for a plausible noun phrase following the main verb that we can use as the unexpressed subject of the infinitive. Here are some examples:

> To lose that contract would be a disaster for our company.

Our company is the default unexpressed subject of *to lose*.

> Just to get the right cable for the printer cost Tom twenty dollars.

Tom is the default unexpressed subject of *to get*.

> To miss an important exam was totally out of character for her.

Her is the default unexpressed subject of *to miss*.

If there is no noun phrase following the main verb that could possibly function as the subject of the infinitive, a likely default interpretation is that the infinitive is being used to make a generalization. For example:

> To be cut off from all human contact is a terrifying prospect.

The most likely interpretation of this sentence is that it is a generalization about what would happen to anybody who is totally cut off from others.

Here are some more examples of subject infinitives being used to make generalizations:

> To become fluent in spoken English takes years.
> To lose a job in this economy is really bad news.

When the infinitive plays the role of object of the verb, the most common default interpretation is that the subject of the main sentence is the unexpressed subject of the infinitive. Here are some examples:

> We need to get some milk at the grocery store.

We is the default unexpressed subject of *get*.

> He always tries to be helpful.

He is the default unexpressed subject of *be*.

Underline the infinitives in the following sentences. Identify the subject using the appropriate default interpretation. If there is no subject, write "generalization." The first question is done as an example.

Roberta started <u>to call the meeting to order.</u>

Roberta is the unexpressed subject of to call.

1. To give up easily suggests a lack of commitment.

   _____

2. She never forgets to thank people who have done her a favor.

   _____

3. To pass the exam on the first try shows that Marion was really prepared.

   _____

4. The trial continued to attract national attention for weeks.

   _____

5. To have this much snow in the mountains means that we may have spring flooding.

   _____

6. Thanks, but some friends offered to drive us to the airport.

   _____

7. To constantly have to add oil means that we should take the car to the garage.

   _____

8. Somehow, John always seems to get his own way.

   _____

9. It is not easy to get old.

   _____

10. It really upset all of us to see the house left in such poor condition.

   _____

Noun clauses

In this chapter we will examine three aspects of noun clauses: (1) where noun clauses can be used, (2) the structure of *that* noun clauses, and (3) the structure of *wh-* noun clauses.

Where noun clauses can be used

Noun clauses are dependent clauses that function as abstract nouns. The two most important types of noun clauses are ***that* clauses** and ***wh-* clauses**. The noun clauses take their names from the first word that begins the clause. *That* clauses, obviously, begin with *that*. *Wh-* clauses are so called because nearly all the first words begin with the letters *wh-*. For example: *who, what, which, when, where,* and *why.* (Strangely enough, there is no standard name in traditional grammar for the *wh-* words that begin noun clauses, possibly because *wh-* words are a mixture of pronouns, e.g., *who,* and adverbs, e.g., *where.*)

Here are some examples of *that* and *wh-* clauses playing the main noun roles:

Subject

That clause:	That I would be chosen came as a complete surprise to me.
Wh- clause:	What he did came as a complete surprise to me.

Object

That clause:	I know that it was a shock.
Wh- clause:	I know what he did came as a shock.

Object of a preposition

That clauses cannot be used as objects of prepositions.

Wh- clause:	I asked him about what had happened.

Predicate nominative

That clause:	The problem was that we didn't have enough time to finish.
Wh- clause:	The question always is how much it will cost.

As the above examples show, we can generally use *that* clauses and *wh-* clauses interchangeably. That is, where we can use one type of noun clause, we expect to be able to use the other types. The one main exception is noun clauses used as objects of prepositions—here only *wh-* clauses can be used.

As we saw in the chapters on gerunds and infinitives, the basic rule is that noun clauses can be used only where we can also use **abstract nouns**. Abstract nouns refer to intangible concepts—as opposed to animate and concrete nouns that refer to living things and objects, respectively. Some useful abstract nouns are *effort, plan, success, idea, cost, problem,* and *outcome.* It is a good bet that wherever you can use one or more of these abstract nouns, you can also use noun clauses. For example, see how all the noun clauses above are used in places where abstract nouns could also be used:

Subject

That clause:	That I would be chosen came as a complete surprise to me.
	The idea
Wh- clause:	What he did came as a complete surprise to me.
	The outcome

Object

That clause:	I know that it was a shock.
	the plan
Wh- clause:	I know what he did came as a shock.
	the problem

Object of a preposition

That clauses cannot be used as objects of prepositions.

Wh- clause:	I asked him about what had happened.
	the problem

Predicate nominative

That-clause:	The problem was that we didn't have enough time to finish.
	the effort
Wh- clause:	The question always is how much it will cost.
	the cost

Each of the following sentences has a blank space where a noun belongs. Use
the test abstract nouns effort, plan, success, idea, cost, problem, or outcome to
determine whether or not noun clauses could be used in that space. If the
abstract nouns do not make sense, write "no noun clause." If they do make sense,
write in one of the test abstract nouns and confirm your answer by writing both
a that clause and a wh- clause in the space provided. (After prepositions, you can
only use wh- noun clauses.) The first question is done as an example.

_____ *The problem* _____ came as a shock to me.

That the test was today came as a shock to me.

What it would cost came as a shock to me.

1. The test results confirmed _____.

   _____

   _____

2. Everybody was surprised by _____.

   _____

   _____

3. Our friends told us _____.

   _____

   _____

4. The proposal attracted _____.

   _____

   _____

5. The funny thing was _____.

   _____

   _____

6. We were all very worried about _____.

_____

_____

7. The angry crowd attacked _____.

_____

_____

8. _____ struck all of us as odd.

_____

_____

9. We need to talk about _____.

_____

_____

10. _____ stepped briskly onto the stage.

_____

_____

There is one additional place where *that* clauses can be used: as the complements of certain predicate adjectives. For example:

> I am happy that things worked out for you.
> The kids were upset that we had to cancel the picnic.
> I am certain that it will be OK.

What makes these particular *that* clauses so unusual is that they do not play a noun role. We cannot replace them with *it*, as we would expect:

> I am happy that things worked out for you.
>   X it
> The kids were upset that we had to cancel the picnic.
>   X it
> I am certain that it will be OK.
>   X it

There are two groups of predicate adjectives that permit *that* clauses. By far the largest group are predicate adjectives that describe an attitude or state of mind. For example: *amused, aware, grateful, surprised, worried.* A much smaller group are predicate adjectives that express certainty. For example: *confident, convinced, sure.*

EXERCISE
15·2

The following sentences all contain that *clauses used as adjective complements. However, some of the adjective complements have been incorrectly used with predicate adjectives that do not accept* that *clause complements. Underline each* that *clause and then label the* that *clause as "grammatical" or "ungrammatical." The first question is done as an example.*

The company was unfair <u>that so many people were laid off.</u>

___*Ungrammatical*___

1. John is always sure that he is right.

   _____

2. I am not happy that things turned out the way they did.

   _____

3. We are ready that it is time to go.

   _____

4. The waiter was positive that I had ordered the seafood special.

   _____

5. The coach was disappointed that the team had made so many mistakes.

   _____

6. I am aware that we made a commitment to them.

   _____

7. The senator was irritated that the reporter had asked such difficult questions.

   _____

8. Frankly, he is still convinced that he did the right thing.

_____

9. The recommendation was vague that the project was going to be approved.

_____

10. He was really hurt that so few people turned up for his retirement party.

_____

That clauses

That clauses (unlike *wh-* clauses) are built in a very simple manner. The introductory word *that* is followed by a statement in normal sentence word order:

> *That* clause = *that* + statement

The simplicity of *that* clauses means that nonnative speakers have relatively few problems with them. Our discussion will focus on two unusual aspects of *that* clauses that do cause problems: deleted *that* and transposed or shifted *that* causes.

Deleted *that*

When *that* clauses are the objects of verbs or the complements of predicate adjectives, *that* is often deleted. (In fact, in conversation *that* is deleted about 75 percent of the time.) For example:

Object of linking verbs
I expect ~~that~~ we will hear from them soon.
He promised ~~that~~ they would give us a call tonight.
I sure wish ~~that~~ it would stop raining.

Complement of predicate adjectives
We are all happy ~~that~~ you are here.
He is convinced ~~that~~ the other driver caused the accident.
I am quite aware ~~that~~ there is a problem.

Deleting the introductory *that* from the beginning of *that* clauses poses a special problem for nonnative speakers because the introductory *that* is the key signal that marks the beginning of a *that* clause. When this flag word is deleted, it is much more difficult to recognize the presence of a *that* clause.

Underline the that *clauses in the following sentences. Confirm your answer by inserting the missing* that. *The first question is done as an example.*

Everyone knew they would have to extend the deadline they initially set.

Everyone knew ***that*** <u>they would have to extend the deadline they initially set</u> .

1. Just pretend you didn't hear what they said.

_____

2. We were worried you didn't get our phone message.

_____

3. I guess you were right after all.

_____

4. I'm not sure we can afford to do it.

_____

5. We all realize the economy is struggling.

_____

6. His parents were grateful he wasn't seriously injured in the accident.

_____

7. You should forget I said anything about it.

_____

8. We insist you all stay for dinner.

_____

9. Everyone is pleased things turned out the way they did in the end.

_____

10. I'm sure they would deny they ever made a mistake.

_____

Transposed or shifted *that* clauses

English speakers are uncomfortable with long or complicated *that* clauses playing the role of subject. In fact 80 percent of the time, subject *that* clauses are transposed or shifted to the end of the sentence. An "empty" or "dummy" *it* is used as a place holder in the now vacated subject position. Here are some examples, first with the *that* clause in its original subject position and then with the *that* clause in its shifted position:

Original	That our team might actually win seemed a miracle.
Shifted	**It** seemed a miracle that our team might actually win.
Original	That the operation was over so quickly came as a big relief.
Shifted	**It** came as a big relief that the operation was over so quickly.

If the main verb in the sentence is a linking verb followed by a predicate adjective that expresses certainty or makes a value statement, then we shift the subject *that* clause nearly 100 percent of the time. For example:

Original	That we were in real trouble became all too clear.
Shifted	**It** became all too clear that we were in real trouble.
Original	That your parents could come for the weekend was nice.
Shifted	**It** was nice that your parents could come for the weekend.

EXERCISE
15·4

Underline subject that *clauses in the following sentences, then shift the subject* that *clauses to the end of the sentence and replace the subject with* it. *The first question is done as an example.*

That tuition costs have risen so much is shocking.

It is shocking that tuition costs have risen so much.

1. That George was going to quit didn't surprise anyone.

2. That humans originated in Africa is now generally accepted.

3. That Alice and Frank broke up came as a big shock to all their friends.

4. That parents understand how to correctly install infant car seats is essential.

5. That I did so well on the project really helped my final grade.

   _____

6. That our costs were getting out of control became increasingly evident.

   _____

7. That he takes such big chances is not OK.

   _____

8. That my driver's license had expired completely escaped my attention.

   _____

9. That they would get upset about it is quite understandable.

   _____

10. That texting while you are driving is really dangerous is common knowledge.

    _____

Wh- clauses

Wh- clauses are noun clauses that begin with *wh-* words. There are two types of *wh-* words: pronouns and adverbs. Most of the *wh-* words also have a compound form ending in *-ever*. Here is the complete list.

Pronouns

who	whoever
whom	whomever
whose	
what	whatever
which	whichever

Adverbs

where	wherever
when	whenever
how	however
how often, how much, how far, how long . . .	
why	

The internal structure of *wh-* clauses is complex. This complexity leads to mistakes because the more complex a grammatical structure is, the more difficult it is for us to monitor that structure for correctness. All noun clauses are difficult because they are abstract sentences embedded as nouns inside another sentence. *Wh-* clauses are especially difficult because *wh-* clauses are formed by a movement rule that shifts the *wh-* word from its normal position to the beginning of the *wh-* clause. This rule is doubly complicated because the movement rule is conditional. That is, under certain conditions the *wh-* word moves and under other conditions it does not move. Most errors involving *wh-* clauses are a direct consequence of the complexities of moving the *wh-* word.

In this discussion we will initially focus on two areas where *wh-* word movement is most likely to cause problems for nonnative speakers (and not a few native speakers as well): *who* or *whom*, and using question word order in *wh-* noun clauses. Finally, we will look at an odd kind of reduced *wh-* noun clauses: *wh-* infinitive phrases.

Who or whom?

Who and *whom* are unique among the *wh-* words in that they have different forms depending on their grammatical role: *who* is used for subjects, and *whom* is used for objects of verbs and objects of prepositions. In discussing *who* and *whom*, we must be careful to distinguish between the role of *who* and *whom* INSIDE the *wh-* clause and the role the entire *wh-* clause plays in the main sentence. To see the problem, ask yourself which of the following sentences is correct—should it be (1) *whoever* or (2) *whomever*?

1. We will be glad to talk to **whoever** shows up at the meeting.

2. We will be glad to talk to **whomever** shows up at the meeting.

The answer is (1) *whoever*. To understand why, we need to think of the *wh-* clause as an island cut off from the rest of the main sentence. On the island, *whoever* is the subject of the verb *shows up*. This subject-verb relationship has nothing to do with anything outside the island. In the main sentence, the verb is *talk to*. The object of the verb *talk to* is the ENTIRE *wh-* noun clause *whoever shows up at the meeting*. In other words, the entire noun clause is a single unit, an island, and this entire island is the object of the main verb, not some particular noun inside the island. The verb *talk to* cannot get onto the island to single out *whomever* to be its object.

A good way to decide between *who* and *whom* is to put parentheses around the *wh-* clause to remind ourselves that it is an island. Looking only inside the island, ask yourself whether the *wh-* word is or is not the subject of the verb inside the island. If it is the subject, the *wh-* word has to be the subject form *who* or *whoever*. If it is not the subject, the *wh-* word has be to the object form *whom* or *whomever*.

Here is an example of this technique:

Did you find out **who/whom** they wanted to talk to?

The first step is to put parentheses around the *wh-* noun clause:

Did you find out (**who/whom** they wanted to talk to)?

Then find out whether or not the *wh-* word is the subject of the verb inside the parentheses. In our example, clearly the *wh-* word is not the subject because the pronoun *they* is. Therefore, we must use *whom* rather than *who*. Note that this test does not need to discover what role the *wh-* word actually plays. All we are interested in is the simple question of whether or not the *wh-* word is the subject. The answer to that question tells us all we need to know to decide between *who* and *whom*.

EXERCISE
15·5

Put parentheses around the entire wh- *clause. Underline the subject of the verb in parentheses. Then cross out the incorrect wh- word. The first question is done as an example.*

I asked (~~who~~/whom <u>he</u> would pick for the job).

1. Did the reporters ever find out who/whom the police arrested?

_____

2. We will help whoever/whomever asks for help.

_____

3. She asked him who/whom he had seen at the reception.

_____

4. I will play whoever/whomever wins the game this afternoon.

_____

5. If I were you I wouldn't care much about who/whom she dated in high school.

_____

6. Whoever/whomever the bride picks will cater the wedding reception.

_____

7. You will have to be whoever/whomever the director casts you as.

_____

8. I just realized who/whom that man was talking about.

_____

9. Whoever/whomever they pick for the job is going to have to do a lot of traveling.

_____

10. They always reserve some seats for whoever/whomever comes into the session late.

_____

Using *wh-* question word order in *wh-* noun clauses

By far the most common error that nonnative speakers make (both beginners and advanced students) is that they use the inverted verb word order of *wh-* questions (also called information questions) in *wh-* noun clauses. Here are some examples:

Wh- question	**Who is** that man?
Incorrect *wh-* clause	X I know **who is** that man.
Correct *wh-*clause	I know **who** that man **is.**
Wh- question	**What was** the problem?
Incorrect *wh-* clause	X I knew **what was** the problem.
Correct *wh-*clause	I knew **what** the problem **was.**
Wh- question	**Where should** we go?
Incorrect *wh-* clause	X I know **where should** we go.
Correct *wh-*clause	I know **where** we **should** go.

As you can see, the difference between *wh-* questions and *wh-* noun clauses in the above examples is that the verb in the *wh-* questions has been moved in front of the subject of the question. In the *wh-* noun clauses, the verb must stay in its normal position following the subject. The simplest way to monitor *wh-* noun clauses is to be sure that the verb FOLLOWS the subject. For example, which of the two *wh-* noun clauses below is wrong and which is correct?

1. I asked them what was the problem.

2. I asked them what the problem was.

Let's look at the word order of the subjects and verbs:

1. I asked them (what <u>was</u> <u>the problem</u>).
                                verb   subject

2. I asked them (what <u>the problem</u> <u>was</u>).
                             subject   verb

Example (1) is incorrect because the verb is in front of the subject. Example (2) is correct because the verb follows the subject.

EXERCISE
15·6

Put parentheses around the wh- noun clauses in the following sentences. Underline and label the subjects and verbs in the wh- noun clauses. If the word order is correct, write "correct." If the word order is wrong, write "incorrect" and make the necessary corrections. The first question is done as an example.

We all wondered (where <u>was</u> <u>the pizza</u> we had ordered).   *Incorrect*

(where the pizza we had ordered was)

1. How should we pay for it was the big question.

_____

2. They wondered where could they find an ATM.

_____

3. Do you know why is it so hot in here?

_____

4. Just listen to what are you saying!

_____

5. The newspapers all reported what Senator Blather said.

_____

6. The judge told the jury what could they consider as evidence.

_____

7. How had they behaved offended everyone there.

_____

8. When was the data collected could make a big difference.

_____

9. I couldn't imagine whom was he talking about.

_____

10. Could you figure out what was he saying?

_____

Wh- infinitive phrases

Infinitive phrases are derived from complete sentences. (See Chapter 14, "Infinitives," for details.) *Wh-* infinitives differ from normal infinitives because *wh-* infinitives are derived from *wh-* noun clauses rather than free-standing complete sentences. To see the relationship of *wh-* noun clauses and *wh-* infinitives, compare the following:

Wh- noun clause:	I didn't know where I should go for help.
Wh- infinitive:	I didn't know where to go for help.

As you can see, the *wh-* infinitive differs from its underlying *wh-* clause in two ways: the subject of the *wh-* clause has been deleted and the tensed verb *should go* has been changed to the infinitive *to go*. Here are some more examples of *wh-* noun clauses and their corresponding *wh-* infinitives playing all the main noun roles:

Subject

Wh- noun clause:	Whom we should invite to a wedding is always a problem.
Wh- infinitive:	Whom to invite to a wedding is always a problem.

Object of a verb

Wh- noun clause:	I didn't know where I should go for help.
Wh- infinitive:	I didn't know where to go for help.

Object of a preposition

Wh- noun clause:	We talked about how we should solve the problem.
Wh- infinitive	We talked about how to solve the problem.

Predicate nominative

Wh- noun clause:	Our immediate problem was how we could start the car.
Wh- infinitive:	Our immediate problem was how to start the car.

Underline the wh- *noun clauses in the following sentences. Rewrite the* wh- *noun clause as a* wh- *infinitive. The first question is done as an example.*

I was really worried about <u>what I should say to her</u>.

I was really worried about _____*what to say to her*_____.

1. Her father showed him how he could replace the window.

   _____

2. I found out where I could get really good pizza.

   _____

3. Where we should go on vacation became a topic for heated debate.

   _____

4. They worried about how much they should charge per hour.

   _____

5. The committee's main concern was whom they should nominate.

   _____

6. The new guidelines spell out what you should do in an emergency.

   _____

7. It is hard to know what one should expect with a group of teenagers.

   _____

8. There were divided opinions on what we should do.

   _____

9. You must choose whom you want to believe.

   _____

10. When we should schedule the conference depends completely on people's schedules.

    _____

Answer key

1   Noun plurals

1·1
1. delays
2. tools
3. stones
4. flies
5. necks
6. switches
7. libraries
8. paths
9. guesses
10. valleys

1·2
1. clocks /s/
2. hedges /əz/
3. colleagues /z/
4. phones /z/
5. allowances /əz/
6. songs /z/
7. rivers /z/
8. moths /s/
9. trees /z/
10. mists /s/
11. garages /əz/
12. boxes /əz/
13. loves /z/
14. tricks /s/
15. zoos /z/

1·3
1. teeth
2. loaves
3. geese
4. shelves
5. oxen
6. trout
7. knives
8. mice
9. wolves
10. cliffs (trick question: the *f* to *v* rule does not apply to *ff*)

1·4
1. stimula
2. memoranda
3. syllabi
4. spectra
5. consortia

1-5　　Abstractions: charity, hope, knowledge; Academic fields: geology, literature; Food: cheese, pepper, rice; Gerunds: laughing, sleeping, talking; Languages: Chinese, Russian; Liquids and gases: beer, coffee, oxygen; Materials: glass, gold, wool; Natural phenomena: gravity, time; Sports and games: football, poker; Weather words: snow, sunshine

2　Possessive nouns and personal pronouns

2·1
1. mouse's; mice; mice's
2. thief's; thieves; thieves'
3. child's; children; children's
4. goose's; geese; geese's
5. ox's; oxen; oxen's
6. deer's; deer; deer's
7. foot's; feet; feet's
8. tooth's; teeth; teeth's
9. fish's; fish; fish's
10. wolf's; wolves; wolves'

2·2
1. it is; it's
2. it is; OK
3. it is; its
4. it is; it's
5. it is; its
6. it is; it's
7. it is; OK
8. it is; its
9. it is; OK
10. it is; it's

2·3
1. a week's postponement (5) measurement
2. Joan's friends (2) association
3. John's interference with another player (4) action
4. Sally's lunch (1) possession
5. the court's refusal (4) action
6. Jason's cheerful nature (3) attribute
7. the couples' friends and relatives (2) association
8. a week's vacation (5) measurement
9. the judge's decisions (4) action
10. everyone's investments (1) possession

2·4
1. the duration of two years
2. ungrammatical
3. the recommendation of the lawyer
4. the status of the yen
5. the runway of the airport
6. ungrammatical
7. ungrammatical
8. ungrammatical
9. the firmness of the tissue
10. ungrammatical

3 Articles and quantifiers

3·1
1. the checks: defined by modifiers
2. the equator: uniqueness
3. the necklace: defined by modifiers
4. the windshield wiper: normal expectations
5. the capital: uniqueness
6. the memo: defined by modifiers
7. the Internet: uniqueness
8. the boat: previous mention
9. the menus: normal expectations
10. the verbs: defined by modifiers
11. the performance: previous mention
12. the bus: defined by modifiers
13. the sand: normal expectations
14. the package: previous mention
15. the mole: defined by modifiers

3·2
1. some rain
2. a note
3. a page
4. some pages
5. some circumstances
6. a reservation
7. some advice
8. a suggestion
9. some disappointment
10. some progress

3·3
1. some reporters
2. any concern
3. some rice
4. any brown rice
5. some big mountains
6. any encouragement
7. some responses
8. any choices
9. some gas
10. any gas

3·4
1. some clean shirts
2. any remorse
3. any impression
4. some errors
5. any idea
6. any passengers
7. some games
8. any ballots
9. any passenger trains
10. some professors

3·5
1. Did they come to any agreement about the contract?
2. Did any cars get stuck in the snow?
3. Are there any direct flights left?
4. Did he order any soup?
5. Was there any frost during the night?
6. She didn't have any congestion this morning.

7. They won't take any time off.

8. There aren't any apartments available.

9. I didn't see any empty boxes at the grocery store.

10. I haven't had any pain in my wrist.

3·6
1. some sunshine: noncategorical
2. sunshine: categorical
3. bridges: categorical
4. assignments: categorical
5. the last assignment: noncategorical
6. engines: categorical
7. location: categorical
8. a new location: noncategorical
9. a freeze: noncategorical
10. failure: categorical

3·7
1. an answer
2. ∅ cheese
3. some cheese
4. ∅ live performances
5. some TV channels
6. ∅ traveling
7. ∅ conferences
8. some locations
9. ∅ sea birds
10. a glass of water

3·8
1. many ducks
2. much coffee
3. many high schools
4. a lot of flu cases
5. much patience
6. many replacement parts
7. much snow
8. a lot of grief
9. much time
10. a lot of concern

3·9
1. little relief
2. any judges
3. few buildings
4. little confidence
5. any food
6. any pictures
7. little assistance
8. any pilots
9. little pride
10. any messages

3·10
1. less pressure
2. fewer job openings
3. less floor space
4. less paperwork
5. less inflation
6. fewer accidents
7. fewer steps
8. less time
9. fewer deaths
10. less light

4 Adjectives

4·1
1. ancient: more/most
2. modern: more/most
3. silly: -er/-est
4. civil: more/most
5. friendly: more/most; -er/-est
6. ready: -er/-est
7. common: more/most
8. dreadful: more/most
9. shallow: -er/-est
10. mindless: more/most
11. private: more/most
12. recent: more/most
13. sincere: more/most
14. tiring: more/most
15. easy: -er/-est

4·2
1. the (~~discouraging~~/discouraged) team
2. a very (tempting/~~tempted~~) offer.
3. the (~~recording~~/recorded) message
4. a new (recording/~~recorded~~) machine
5. a (~~respecting~~/respected) lawyer
6. a (~~deserting~~/deserted) island
7. a very (moving/~~moved~~) speech
8. Napoleon's (retreating/~~retreated~~) army
9. the (~~restricting~~/restricted) area
10. the (existing/~~existed~~) building
11. the (striking/~~struck~~) employees
12. the (~~damaging~~/damaged) curtains
13. a (passing/~~passed~~) taxi
14. a very (encouraging/~~encouraged~~) response
15. the (~~attempting~~/attempted) coup

5 Verb forms and tenses

5·1
1. will be cleaning
2. have stayed
3. were attracting
4. will be expanding
5. had adopted
6. will be emerging
7. should be delivering
8. might have heard
9. are threatening
10. couldn't have seen

5·2
1. had been proposing
2. has been affecting
3. will have been claiming
4. had been repairing
5. had been issuing
6. have been having
7. had been hoping
8. should have been preparing
9. might have been staying
10. have been having

5·3	1. present progressive	6. simple present
	2. present perfect	7. future perfect progressive
	3. future progressive	8. present perfect
	4. past perfect progressive	9. present perfect progressive
	5. future progressive	10. future progressive

5·4
1. should have been (future perfect)
2. will be continuing (future progressive)
3. must have been (future perfect)
4. have been hearing (present perfect progressive)
5. must be talking (future progressive)
6. have been having (present perfect progressive)
7. should have been studying (future perfect progressive)
8. have been being (present perfect progressive)
9. should have had (future perfect)
10. might have been being (future perfect progressive)

6 Talking about present time

6·1	1. She misses	6. He always enjoys
	2. You are missing	7. I am coming down
	3. He is avoiding	8. We are thinking
	4. Her company publishes	9. He always puts on
	5. She is teaching	10. I am facing

6·2	1. Exercise **reduces** (assertion)	6. they **drive** (fact)
	2. moon **determines** (fact)	7. People seldom **save** (assertion)
	3. Health insurance **costs** (assertion)	8. increase in inflation **proves** (assertion)
	4. We always **get** (habitual)	9. we **watch** (habitual)
	5. Water **covers** (fact)	10. A decision by the supreme court **binds** (fact)

6·3	1. am counting	6. is examining
	2. dislikes: stative	7. consists: stative
	3. is threatening	8. is reviewing
	4. want: stative	9. contains: stative
	5. is finding	10. know: stative

6·4
1. states: narrative
2. begins: narrative
3. closes: future
4. ends: narrative
5. are: narrative
6. spend: future
7. close: narrative
8. is: future
9. is: narrative
10. sets: future

6·5
1. ungrammatical
2. They **have studied** together all this semester.
3. The company **has lost** money ever since the recession began.
4. ungrammatical
5. We **have** always **discussed** our differences openly.
6. They **have worked** on the project ever since it was first approved.
7. ungrammatical
8. ungrammatical
9. ungrammatical
10. They **have** always **argued** over it.

6·6
1. has collected: (3) completed action
2. has administered: (1) continuous activity
3. have spoken: (2) immediate past action
4. has fixed: (1) continuous activity
5. has stepped: (2) immediate past action
6. have accomplished: (3) completed action
7. has rained: (1) continuous activity
8. has kept: (3) completed action
9. have urged: (1) continuous activity
10. have figured: (2) immediate past action

7 Talking about past time

7·1
1. knit
2. cut
3. fit
4. quit
5. let
6. split
7. shut
8. wet
9. bid
10. rid

7·2
1. turned: past time
2. could: polite
3. graduated: past time
4. were: hypothetical
5. didn't: past time
6. did: polite
7. got: hypothetical
8. concluded: past time
9. quit: hypothetical
10. could: polite

7·3
1. ~~closed~~ had closed
2. ~~was~~ had been
3. ~~used~~ had used
4. ~~confirmed~~ had already confirmed
5. ~~made~~ had made
6. ~~closed~~ had already closed
7. ~~spent~~ had already spent
8. ~~looked~~ had looked
9. ~~made~~ had made
10. ~~come~~ had come

8 Talking about future time

8·1
1. shouldn't <u>fear</u>: main verb
2. must <u>have</u> adjusted: perfect helping verb
3. I'll <u>have</u>: main verb
4. will <u>be</u> retiring: progressive helping verb
5. must <u>have</u> noticed: perfect helping verb
6. will <u>invite</u>: main verb
7. will <u>be</u>: main verb
8. must <u>be</u> going: progressive helping verb
9. will <u>have</u> cost: perfect helping verb
10. might <u>be</u> dropping: progressive helping verb

8·2
1. may: (1) prediction
2. may: (4) permission/request
3. can: (5) capability
4. might: (1) prediction
5. should: (2) obligation
6. should: (1) prediction
7. must: (3) necessity, but also: (2) obligation
8. shall: (4) permission/request
9. may: (5) capability
10. won't: (1) prediction

8·3
1. you **can** do it.
2. devices **should** meet
3. we **will** meet
4. it **might** rain
5. they **could** make
6. I **would** be happy
7. you **may** go outside
8. devices **shall** meet
9. animals **can** take care
10. We **will** keep

8·4   1. storm is drifting

  2. he is coming

  3. Christmas falls

  4. I am taking

  5. none

  6. When does the office open?

  7. banks close

  8. they are catching

  9. none

  10. we are getting

9 Causative verbs

9·1   1. raising tobacco

  2. rise before noon

  3. rates have been rising

  4. raise the money

  5. raised the anchor

  6. raised in California (passive)

  7. raise the ceiling

  8. rising tide (adjective derived from present participle)

  9. skirt length rises

  10. eyebrows were raised (passive)

9·2   1. please sit

  2. set my keys

  3. sit next to the door

  4. have not been set (passive)

  5. I'm sitting

  6. the fort sits

  7. set the coffee

  8. his face set (passive)

  9. everyone was sitting

  10. Has the agenda been set? (passive)

9·3   1. lie back

  2. had lain

  3. she laid

  4. had been laid (passive)

  5. was lying

  6. must lay

  7. town lies

  8. best laid plans

  9. he lay back

  10. have been lying around

9·4   1. to turn

  2. to take

  3. hurry

  4. to brush

  5. return

  6. to reject

  7. be

  8. to pull

  9. trim

  10. do

10 The passive

10·1 1. were helping: the past participle verb form is missing

2. had been met: passive

3. has appeared: *be* as a helping verb is missing

4. will be continued: passive

5. have learned: *be* as a helping verb is missing

6. should have been taken: passive

7. are making: the past participle verb form is missing

8. must have been lost: passive

9. are carrying: the past participle verb form is missing

10. will be believed: passive

10·2 1. An answer <u>will</u> <u>be</u> <u>wanted</u> by them immediately.

     pres base past
       form part

2. A new pet <u>is</u> <u>being</u> <u>chosen</u> by the kids.

    pres base past
      form part

3. The data <u>has</u> <u>been</u> <u>entered</u> in the wrong column by them.

    pres past past
      part part

4. The accident <u>should</u> <u>have</u> <u>been</u> <u>investigated</u> by the police.

     past base past past
       form part part

5. A new offer <u>has</u> <u>been</u> <u>made</u> by them.

    pres past past
      part part

6. Too much time <u>is</u> <u>being</u> <u>lost</u> by them.

     pres pres past
       part part

7. The meeting <u>could</u> <u>have</u> <u>been</u> <u>postponed</u> by them.

     past base past past
       form part part

8. The car <u>will</u> not <u>be</u> <u>being</u> <u>used</u> by me tomorrow.
                pres   form part part
                base   pres past

9. A new motion <u>might</u> <u>have</u> <u>been</u> <u>filed</u> by their lawyers.
                  past   base past past
                        form part part

10. The train <u>should</u> <u>have</u> <u>been</u> <u>taken</u> by them.
                past   base past past
                     form part part

10·3
1. have been issued: (2) impersonal entity or institution
2. was made: (1) unknown or unknowable agent
3. has been sent: (4) agent withheld because embarrassing or awkward
4. is often misspelled: (3) universal or generalized agent
5. had been covered: (1) unknown or unknowable agent
6. were always told: (3) universal or highly generalized agent
7. has been rejected: (4) agent withheld because embarrassing or awkward
8. is more often praised: (3) universal or highly generalized
9. has been closed: (2) impersonal entity or institution
10. was filmed: (1) unknown or unknowable agent

10·4
1. The doctor offered several alternative treatments.
2. The children had grown the tomatoes in our garden.
3. The Chief Justice was administering the oath of office.
4. Everyone had learned a valuable lesson.
5. The people in the neighborhood should have alerted the police.
6. An MRI scan first identified the tumor.
7. A large corporation was buying out the company.
8. The local paper would have covered the accident.
9. Fortunately, the Coast Guard rescued the crew.
10. Someone had forced open the door during the night.

10·5   1. I got selected to give the introduction.

2. ungrammatical

3. All of us got sunburned on our camping trip.

4. They got pulled out of the ditch by a tow truck.

5. ungrammatical

6. Did all of the items get sold?

7. ungrammatical

8. Didn't their e-mail get answered?

9. Did she get hurt in the accident?

10. ungrammatical

11   The structure of adjective clauses

11·1   1. Use the desk (**that**) is next to the window for now.

2. I finally got the mosquito (**that**) had bothered me all night.

3. We searched for a place (**where**) we could cross the river.

4. I wanted you to meet the people (**who**) were so helpful during the power outage.

5. Let's pick a time (**when**) we can all meet.

6. I can't stand the sugary cereal (**that**) the kids eat.

7. I only know the people in the building (**who**) work in finance.

8. My parents live in a little town (**where**) everyone knows everyone else.

9. The symptoms (**that**) I had were pretty typical.

10. It was a period (**when**) everything seemed to go wrong all at once.

11·2
1. whom: object
2. whose: possessive
3. that: subject
4. where: spatial
5. that: object of preposition
6. that: object
7. who: subject
8. whose: possessive
9. that: object of preposition
10. that: object

11·3   1. We learned that from the students **whom** we met on the campus tour.

2. The police were searching the area **where** the campers had last been seen.

3. I remember the day **when** she was born.

4. He is a person **whom** one could always turn to.

5. I will introduce you to the teacher **whose** class you will be taking.

6. Two thousand three was the year **when** they were married.

7. Do you know the place **where** they are planning to meet?

8. Unfortunately, he is a man **whom** no one can depend on.

9. She is the author **whose** book we are reading in my literature class.

10. They visited Sutter's Mill **where** gold was first discovered in California.

11·4

1. We really like the color **that** you painted the living room.

2. The children **whom** we saw must belong to the couple next door.

3. The time **when** we were supposed to meet will not work after all.

4. The food **that** they serve in the cafeteria would choke a goat.

5. Everyone hopes that the place **where** we want to meet is still available.

6. We talked to the young couple **whom** you told us about.

7. The defense challenged the evidence **that** the prosecution presented at the trial.

8. They were happy to accept the offer **that** we had agreed on.

9. The dean congratulated the seniors **whom** the department chairs had nominated.

10. We ended up buying the place **where** the real estate agent had taken us.

11·5

1. The gate **that** we had driven through earlier was closed by the police. The gate **through which** we had driven earlier was closed by the police.

2. The story **that** we reported on last night has become national news. The story **on which** we reported last night has become national news.

3. The people **whom** we made friends with invited us over for dinner. The people **with whom** we made friends invited us over for dinner.

4. We made an offer on the apartment **that** we looked at yesterday. We made an offer on the apartment **at which** we looked yesterday.

5. We finally resolved the issues **that** we had been fighting about for some time. We finally resolved the issued **about which** we had been fighting for some time.

6. We had to reconsider the items **that** we had not budgeted for. We had to reconsider the items **for which** we had not budgeted.

7. He was finally given the reward **that** he was entitled to. He was finally given the reward **to which** he was entitled.

8. I brought up the issues **that** we had talked about before. I brought up the issues **about which** we had talked before.

9. We went back to the doctor **whom** we had previously consulted with. We went back to the doctor **with whom** we had previously consulted.

10. We bought the house **that** my parents had lived in. We bought the house **in which** my parents had lived.

12 Restrictive and nonrestrictive adjective clauses

12·1
1. Nonrest: My car, <u>which is fifteen years old</u>, has . . .
2. Rest: The car <u>that is in front of us</u> is leaking oil badly.
3. Nonrest: . . . father, <u>who seemed very anxious to talk to you.</u>
4. Nonrest: . . . my high school math teacher, <u>whom I hadn't seen in years.</u>
5. Rest: The math teacher <u>who taught me algebra in the ninth grade</u> did . . .
6. Nonrest: The Congo River, <u>which crosses the equator twice</u>, flows . . .
7. Rest: There is only one man in town <u>who can repair foreign cars.</u>
8. Rest: The people <u>whom we met at lunch</u> seemed very nice.
9. Rest: The town <u>where they live</u> is about . . .
10. Nonrest: A police officer, <u>who seemed to come out of nowhere</u>, stopped . . .

12·2
1. The first layer of paint, **which** was a white undercoat, dried in less than an hour.
2. The snowstorm ∅ we had been worrying about turned out to be nothing.
3. He called a meeting **that** is in conflict with an important client session.
4. The mouse came out of a hole ∅ I had never even noticed before.
5. My workday, **which** was pretty long to begin with, was extended thirty minutes.
6. His temperature, **which** had now climbed to 103 degrees, was beginning to scare us.
7. We need to rent a truck **that** is big enough to hold all this stuff.
8. During the concert, my cell phone, **which** I had forgotten to turn off, rang loudly.
9. He swatted hopelessly at a mosquito **that** was buzzing around our heads.
10. The only menus ∅ the restaurant had were in Italian.

12·3
1. The course, ~~which is~~ required for all new employees, is offered every month.
2. The books ~~that are~~ required for the course may be purchased at the office.
3. Drivers ~~who are~~ renewing their licenses after January 1 must take an eye exam.
4. We talked to the reporter ~~who was~~ covering the story.
5. All of the children ~~who were~~ born after 2004 have been vaccinated.
6. He is always looking for stocks ~~that are~~ selling at historically low prices.
7. The company, ~~which was~~ once nearly destroyed by labor disputes, is now doing well.
8. The mechanic found the problem ~~that was~~ causing the car to suddenly lose power.
9. Sunlight ~~that was~~ reflected off the building was blinding drivers on the highway.
10. Her first book, ~~which was~~ published when she was only twenty, became a bestseller.

1. The new apple, <u>developed to be pest-resistant</u>, has proved a commercial success. <u>Developed to be pest-resistant</u>, the new apple has proved a commercial success.

2. Many college students, <u>living on their own for the first time</u>, incur far too much debt. <u>Living on their own for the first time</u>, many college students incur far too much debt.

3. She, <u>rushing to answer the phone</u>, slipped on the rug and fell. <u>Rushing to answer the phone</u>, she slipped on the rug and fell.

4. Someone <u>walking past the house</u> noticed the smoke. Cannot move: restrictive participial phrase

5. I, <u>having no background in the matter whatsoever</u>, stayed out the debate. <u>Having no background in the matter whatsoever</u>, I stayed out of the debate.

6. Children <u>just beginning to walk</u> cannot be left alone for a minute. Cannot move: restrictive participial phrase

7. The man, <u>stopping dead in his tracks</u>, stared at us in amazement. <u>Stopping dead in his tracks</u>, the man stared at us in amazement.

8. A person <u>involved in the dispute</u> cannot offer an impartial opinion. Cannot move: restrictive participial phrase

9. We, <u>presented with such an unusual opportunity</u>, decided to act at once. <u>Presented with such an unusual opportunity</u>, we decided to act at once.

10. The police, <u>acting on an anonymous tip</u>, arrested the gang leader. <u>Acting on an anonymous tip</u>, the police arrested the gang leader.

13 Gerunds

Note: Confirmation answers will vary.

1. Gerund: **The outcome** proved that we were capable of doing the job. Confirmation: <u>**Winning the contract**</u> proved that we were capable of doing the job.

2. No gerund: X **The outcome** wished that we had more time.

3. Gerund: They need to encourage **success.** Confirmation: They need to encourage <u>**finishing their work on time.**</u>

4. Gerund: I am very worried about **the outcome**. Confirmation: I am very worried about **having** <u>so much to do.</u>

5. No gerund: X John offered to drive **the problem** to the airport.

6. Gerund: Can you explain **the problem**? Confirmation: Can you explain <u>**missing** such an obvious opportunity?</u>

7. Gerund: We fully support **the effort**. Confirmation: We fully support <u>**seeing** the dentist on a regular basis.</u>

8. Gerund: I argued against **the idea.** Confirmation: I argued against **cutting** the budget so much.

9. No gerund: X The kids ate **success** for breakfast this morning.

10. Gerund: The media dismissed **the idea** as unimportant. Confirmation: The media dismissed **passing** the reform act as unimportant.

13·2
1. <u>Finishing my thesis on time</u> required some real sacrifices.
   It

2. You need to think about <u>taking some time off</u>.
   it

3. I really enjoy <u>working in my garden</u>.
   it

4. He insisted on <u>paying the bill</u>.
   it

5. They are not happy about <u>having to attend a seven o'clock meeting</u>.
   it

6. <u>Enjoying one's work</u> is the key to job satisfaction.
   It

7. I couldn't stand <u>taking all those statistics classes</u>.
   it

8. He felt a lot better after <u>taking a nap</u>.
   it

9. <u>Taking Latin</u> is really good for <u>improving one's vocabulary</u>.
   It   it

10. <u>Getting the early flight</u> will avoid <u>getting stuck in traffic</u>.
    It   it

13·3
1. Every CEO's dream is <u>beating performance expectations</u>.
   Answer: Gerund

   It substitution test: Every CEO's dream is <u>beating performance expectations</u>.
                                                                            it

   every CEO's dream = beating performance expectations

   Past-tense sub test: X Every CEO's dream beat performance expectations.

2. My English assignment is <u>summarizing a chapter of the book</u>.

    Answer: Gerund

    It substitution test: My English assignment is <u>summarizing a chapter of the book</u>.

    it

    my English assignment = summarizing a chapter of the book

    Past-tense sub test: X My English assignment summarized a chapter of the book.

3. A concern of every city in the Southwest is <u>getting enough water</u>.

    Answer: Gerund

    It substitution test: A concern of every city in the Southwest is <u>getting enough water</u>.

    it

    a concern of every city in the Southwest = getting enough water

    Past-tense sub test: X A concern of every city in the Southwest got enough water.

4. John is <u>getting pretty good at playing tennis</u>.

    Answer: Progressive

    It substitution test: John is <u>getting pretty good at playing tennis</u>.

    X it

    X John = getting pretty good at playing tennis

    Past-tense sub test: John got pretty good at playing tennis.

5. My problem is <u>remembering everything I am supposed to do</u>.

    Answer: Gerund

    It substitution test: My problem is <u>remembering everything I am supposed to do</u>.

    it

    my problem = remembering everything I am supposed to do

    Past-tense sub test: X My problem remembered everything I am supposed to do.

6. Most American companies are <u>providing adequate health insurance</u>.

    Answer: Progressive

    It substitution test: Most American companies are <u>providing adequate health insurance</u>.

    X it

    X most American companies = providing adequate health insurance

    Past-tense sub test: Most American companies provided adequate health insurance.

7. Their great concern is <u>providing adequate health insurance</u>.

Answer: Gerund

It substitution test: Their great concern is <u>providing adequate health insurance</u>.

it

their great concern = providing adequate health insurance

Past-tense sub test: X Their great concern provided adequate health insurance.

8. A coach's responsibility is <u>getting the athletes in good condition</u>.

Answer: Gerund

It substitution test: A coach's responsibility is <u>getting the athletes in good condition</u>.

it

a coach's responsibility = getting the athletes in good condition

Past-tense sub test: X A coach's responsibility got the athletes in good condition.

9. A big part of an office manager's job is <u>ordering supplies</u>.

Answer: Gerund

It substitution test: A big part of an office manager's job is <u>ordering supplies</u>.

it

a big part of an office manager's job = ordering supplies

Past-tense sub test: X A big part of an office manager's job ordered supplies.

10. Our office manager is <u>thinking about getting new computers</u>.

Answer: Progressive

It substitution test: Our office manager is <u>thinking about getting new computers</u>.

X it

X our office manager = thinking about getting new computers

Past-tense sub test: Our office manager thought about getting new computers.

13·4   1. (The bank approves the loan) made it possible for us to go ahead.
Step 1: (The bank approving the loan) made it possible for us to go ahead.
Step 2: The bank's approving the loan made it possible for us to go ahead.

2. Everyone resented (he unfairly criticized the school board).
Step 1: Everyone resented (he unfairly criticizing the school board).
Step 2: Everyone resented his unfairly criticizing the school board.

3. We were delayed by (the children needed to take an afternoon nap).
Step 1: We were delayed by (the children needing to take an afternoon nap).
Step 2: We were delayed by the children's needing to take an afternoon nap.

4. (The defendant told a convincing story) persuaded the jury that he was innocent.
   Step 1: (The defendant telling a convincing story) persuaded the jury that he was innocent.
   Step 2: The defendant's telling a convincing story persuaded the jury that he was innocent.

5. What made her so successful was (she was such a good listener).
   Step 1: What made her so successful was (she being such a good listener).
   Step 2: What made her so successful was her being such a good listener.

6. Try to ignore (they behaved so rudely).
   Step 1: Try to ignore (they behaving so rudely).
   Step 2: Try to ignore their behaving so rudely.

7. The odds against (he wins the election) were pretty big.
   Step 1: The odds against (he winning the election) were pretty big.
   Step 2: The odds against his winning the election were pretty big.

8. The campers barely survived (they got lost in the woods).
   Step 1: The campers barely survived (they getting lost in the woods).
   Step 2: The campers barely survived their getting lost in the woods.

9. (I became sick) nearly spoiled our vacation.
   Step 1: (I becoming sick) nearly spoiled our vacation.
   Step 2: My becoming sick nearly spoiled our vacation.

10. We all have to get used to (our children grow up and leave home).
   Step 1: We all have to get used to (our children growing up and leaving home).
   Step 2: We all have to get used to our children's growing up and leaving home.

13·5
1. Getting it right the first time is the main goal. Generalization

2. Running twenty miles a week really helped Sam lose weight. *Sam (Sam's)* is the unexpressed subject of the gerund

3. Complaining about the weather all the time is pointless. Generalization

4. Talking to Bob about his children's bad behavior only makes him angry at us. *Us (our)* is the unexpressed subject of the gerund

5. Having to commute hours each way is really hard on a family. Generalization

6. Trying to please everybody got her into a lot of trouble. *Her* is the unexpressed subject of the gerund

7. Going back to school for a master's degree is one of George's options. *George's* is the unexpressed subject of the gerund

8. Training one's replacement is something that all good administrators should do. Generalization

9. Improving her GPA was Julie's main reason for going to summer school. *Julie's* is the unexpressed subject of the gerund

10. Publishing papers is a major part of being a university professor these days. Generalization

1. I deeply regretted **going back** on my promise to them.
2. The ad promoted families' **choosing** a healthier diet.
3. Her family was pleased with Mary's **getting** her degree.
4. I concentrated on **keeping** just the right tension on the kite string.
5. We approved of his **ordering** pizza for the kids.
6. I asked my advisor about **going** to business school next year.
7. We certainly appreciated **getting** such good service.
8. The kids sensed our **beginning** to get worried about the storm.
9. Everyone predicted our team's **winning** the championship.
10. The canoe race totally depended on the river's **having** enough water.

14 Infinitives

1. The angry citizens demanded to talk to the mayor.

     it **noun**

2. CNN just announced her to be the winner.

     X it **not a noun**

3. We are pleased to welcome our distinguished visitors.

     X it **not a noun**

4. To really learn English grammar takes a lot of time.

     It **noun**

5. There seems to have been a mistake.

     X it **not a noun**

6. We will be sad to leave such a nice place.

     X it **not a noun**

7. The storm caused the river to flood over its banks.

     X it **not a noun**

8. We decided to take her parents out to dinner.

     it **noun**

9. I am not prepared to answer your questions at this time.

     X it **not a noun**

10. Our original idea was to stay home and order some Chinese food.

     it **noun**

14·2   1. <u>To drive a heavy truck</u> requires a special driver's license.

                 It **subject**

      2. I really wanted <u>to believe that everything would work out OK</u>.

                             it **object**

      3. Our first class assignment was <u>to determine how much a small company was worth</u>.

                                 it **predicate nominative**

      4. I decided <u>to take the calculus course after all</u>.

                     it **object**

      5. <u>To teach in middle school</u> requires a person who really likes kids.

                 It **subject**

      6. I don't want <u>to give up so easily</u>.

                    it **object**

      7. <u>To get a new car</u> would be more than we could afford right now.

              It **subject**

      8. I am not ready <u>to go to bed yet</u>.

                   X it **not a noun**

      9. Our main concern is <u>to keep our costs down as much as humanly possible</u>.

                         it **predicate nominative**

    10. We need <u>to get ready</u> <u>to go</u>.

                   it **object**   X it **not a noun**

14·3   1. Our final option was (the contractor replaces the entire front porch).
        Step 1: Our final option was (the contractor to replace the entire front porch).
        Step 2: Our final option was <u>for the contractor to replace the entire front porch</u>.

      2. We would prefer (the children attend the after-school program).
        Step 1: We would prefer (the children to attend the after-school program).
        Step 2: We would prefer <u>for the children to attend the after-school program</u>.

      3. (The company ignores state regulations) was a serious error.
        Step 1: (The company to ignore state regulations) was a serious error.
        Step 2: <u>For the company to ignore state regulations</u> was a serious error.

      4. John would hate (my friends are disappointed).
        Step 1: John would hate (my friends to be disappointed).
        Step 2: John would hate <u>for my friends to be disappointed</u>.

      5. Our greatest fear would be (the pipes in our house froze while we were away).
        Step 1: Our greatest fear would be (the pipes in our house to freeze while we were away).
        Step 2: Our greatest fear would be <u>for the pipes in our house to freeze while we were away</u>.

6. (They take charge like that) really helped us a lot.
   Step 1: (They to take charge like that) really helped us a lot.
   Step 2: For them to take charge like that really helped us a lot.

7. Most parents intend (their children inherit the parents' estate).
   Step 1: Most parents intend (their children to inherit the parents' estate).
   Step 2: Most parents intend for their children to inherit the parents' estate.

8. The plan was (we flew directly back after the conference was over).
   Step 1: The plan was (we to fly directly back after the conference was over).
   Step 2: The plan was for us to fly directly back after the conference was over.

9. (They got so upset over what happened) made everyone quite uncomfortable.
   Step 1: (They to get so upset over what happened) made everyone quite uncomfortable.
   Step 2: For them to get so upset over what happened made everyone quite uncomfortable.

10. The farmers were all praying (the rain came in time to save the crops).
    Step 1: The farmers were all praying (the rain to come in time to save the crops).
    Step 2: The farmers were all praying for the rain to come in time to save the crops.

14·4

1. For us to accept the offer made perfect economic sense. It made perfect economic sense for us to accept the offer.

2. For them not to finish the job on time would be very costly. It would be very costly for them not to finish the job on time.

3. For us to get an independent assessment of the costs seemed only prudent. It seemed only prudent for us to get an independent assessment of the costs.

4. To have a very low voter turnout was Senator Blather's only hope. It was Senator Blather's only hope to have a very low voter turnout.

5. For the whole family to go skiing at a resort would cost an arm and a leg. It would cost an arm and a leg for the whole family to go skiing at a resort.

6. To keep the house clean with children and pets takes a lot of work. It takes a lot of work to keep the house clean with children and pets.

7. For him to say such a thing struck us as very strange. It struck us as very strange for him to say such a thing.

8. For our company to go so deeply into debt worried everyone. It worried everyone for our company to go so deeply into debt.

9. To contest the mayor's decision in court would take a lot of time and effort. It would take a lot of time and effort to contest the mayor's decision in court.

10. For us to lose the first two games would put us in an impossible position. It would put us in an impossible position for us to lose the first two games.

14·5
1. <u>To give up easily</u> suggests a lack of commitment. Generalization
2. She never forgets <u>to thank people who have done her a favor</u>. *She* is the unexpressed subject of *to thank*.
3. <u>To pass the exam on the first try</u> shows that Marion was really prepared. *Marion* is the unexpressed subject of *to pass*.
4. The trial continued <u>to attract national attention for weeks</u>. *The trial* is the unexpressed subject of *to attract*.
5. <u>To have this much snow in the mountains</u> means that we may have spring flooding. *We* is the unexpressed subject of *to have*.
6. Thanks, but some friends offered <u>to drive us to the airport</u>. *Some friends* is the unexpressed subject of *to drive*.
7. <u>To constantly have to add oil</u> means that we should take the car to the garage. *We* is the unexpressed subject of *to have*.
8. Somehow, John always seems <u>to get his own way</u>. *John* is the unexpressed subject of *to get*.
9. It is not easy <u>to get old</u>. The underlying sentence is *To get old is not easy*. Generalization
10. It really upset all of us <u>to see the house left in such poor condition</u>. The underlying sentence is *To see the house left in such poor condition really upset all of us. All of us* is the unexpressed subject of *to see*.

15 Noun clauses

15·1 Note: Confirmation answers will vary.

1. The test results confirmed <u>the outcome</u>. Confirmation: The tests results confirmed <u>that we had a problem</u>. The test results confirmed <u>what we had all expected</u>.
2. Everybody was surprised by <u>the idea</u>. Confirmation: Everybody was surprised by <u>what the answer was</u>.
3. Our friends told us <u>the plan</u>. Confirmation: Our friends told us <u>that they would meet us for dinner</u>. Our friends told us <u>where we should go</u>.
4. The proposal attracted <u>No noun clause</u>.
5. The funny thing was <u>the idea</u>. Confirmation: The funny thing was <u>that we had been right all along</u>. The funny thing was <u>how many people actually showed up</u>.
6. We were all very worried about <u>the cost</u>. Confirmation: We were all very worried about <u>what people would say</u>.
7. The angry crowd attacked <u>No noun clause</u>
8. The outcome struck all of us as odd. Confirmation: <u>That nobody noticed the problem before</u> struck all of us as odd. <u>How everybody responded</u> struck all of us as odd.
9. We need to talk about <u>the problem</u>. Confirmation: We need to talk about <u>what happened last night</u>.
10. <u>No noun clause</u> stepped briskly onto the stage.

15·2   1. John is always sure that he is right. Grammatical

2. I am not happy that things turned out the way they did. Grammatical

3. We are ready that it is time to go. Ungrammatical

4. The waiter was positive that I had ordered the seafood special. Grammatical

5. The coach was disappointed that the team had made so many mistakes. Grammatical

6. I am aware that we made a commitment to them. Grammatical

7. The senator was irritated that the reporter had asked such difficult questions. Grammatical

8. Frankly, he is still convinced that he did the right thing. Grammatical

9. The recommendation was vague that the project was going to be approved. Ungrammatical

10. He was really hurt that so few people turned up for his retirement party. Grammatical

15·3   1. Just pretend **that** you didn't hear what they said.

2. We were worried **that** you didn't get our phone message.

3. I guess **that** you were right after all.

4. I'm not sure **that** we can afford to do it.

5. We all realize **that** the economy is struggling.

6. His parents were grateful **that** he wasn't seriously injured in the accident.

7. You should forget **that** I said anything about it.

8. We insist **that** you all stay for dinner.

9. Everyone is pleased **that** things turned out the way **that** they did in the end.

10. I'm sure **that** they would deny **that** they ever made a mistake.

15·4   1. That George was going to quit didn't surprise anyone. It didn't surprise anyone that George was going to quit.

2. That humans originated in Africa is now generally accepted. It is now generally accepted that humans originated in Africa.

3. That Alice and Frank broke up came as a big shock to all their friends. It came as a big shock to all their friends that Alice and Frank broke up.

4. That parents understand how to correctly install infant car seats is essential. It is essential that parents understand how to correctly install infant car seats.

5. That I did so well on the project really helped my final grade. It really helped my final grade that I did so well on the project.

6. That our costs were getting out of control became increasingly evident. It became increasingly evident that our costs were getting out of control.

7. That he takes such big chances is not OK. It is not OK that he takes such big chances.

8. That my driver's license had expired completely escaped my attention. It completely escaped my attention that my driver's license had expired.

9. That they would get upset about it is quite understandable. It is quite understandable that they would get upset about it.

10. That texting while you are driving is really dangerous is common knowledge. It is common knowledge that texting while you are driving is really dangerous.

15·5
1. Did the reporters ever find out (~~who~~/whom the police arrested)?

2. We will help (whoever/~~whomever~~ asks for help).

3. She asked him (~~who~~/whom he had seen at the reception).

4. I will play (whoever/~~whomever~~ wins the game this afternoon).

5. If I were you I wouldn't care much about (~~who~~/whom she dated in high school).

6. (~~Whoever~~/whomever the bride picks) will cater the wedding reception.

7. You will have to be (~~whoever~~/whomever the director casts you as).

8. I just realized (~~who~~/whom that man was talking about).

9. (~~Whoever~~/whomever they pick for the job) is going to have to do a lot of traveling.

10. They always reserve some seats for (whoever/~~whomever~~ comes into the session late).

15·6
1. (How should we pay for it) was the big question. Incorrect. (How we should pay for it)

2. They wondered (where could they find an ATM). Incorrect. (where they could find an ATM)

3. Do you know (why is it so hot in here)? Incorrect. (why it is so hot in here)

4. Just listen to (what are you saying)! Incorrect. (what you are saying)

5. The newspapers all reported (what Senator Blather said). Correct.

6. The judge told the jury (what could they consider as evidence). Incorrect. (what they could consider as evidence)

7. (How had they behaved) offended everyone there. Incorrect. (How they had behaved)

8. (When was the data collected) could make a big difference. Incorrect. (When the data was collected)

9. I couldn't imagine (whom was he talking about). Incorrect. (whom he was talking about)

10. Could you figure out (what was he saying)? Incorrect. (what he was saying)

15·7 1. Her father showed him <u>how he could replace the window</u>. Her father showed him <u>how to replace the window</u>.

2. I found out <u>where I could get really good pizza</u>. I found out <u>where to get really good pizza</u>.

3. <u>Where we should go on vacation</u> became a topic for heated debate. <u>Where to go on vacation</u> became a topic for heated debate.

4. They worried about <u>how much they should charge per hour</u>. They worried about <u>how much to charge per hour</u>.

5. The committee's main concern was <u>whom they should nominate</u>. The committee's main concern was <u>whom to nominate</u>.

6. The new guidelines spell out <u>what you should do in an emergency</u>. The new guidelines spell out <u>what to do in an emergency</u>.

7. It is hard to know <u>what one should expect with a group of teenagers</u>. It is hard to know <u>what to expect with a group of teenagers</u>.

8. There were divided opinions on <u>what we should do</u>. There were divided opinions on <u>what to do</u>.

9. You must choose <u>whom you want to believe</u>. You must choose <u>whom to believe</u>.

10. <u>When we should schedule the conference</u> depends completely on people's schedules. <u>When to schedule the conference</u> depends completely on people's schedules.

About the Author

Mark Lester is an experienced grammarian, ESL expert, and emeritus college professor. He was the founding chair of the ESL department at the University of Hawaii, which is considered one of the best ESL programs in the United States. He is the author of more than a dozen books, including the widely used *Grammar and Usage in the Classroom*. For McGraw-Hill Professional, he authored *McGraw-Hill's Essential ESL Grammar* and *English Grammar Drills*, and he coauthored *The McGraw-Hill Handbook of English Grammar and Usage* (with Larry Beason), *The Big Book of English Verbs*, and *McGraw-Hill's Essential English Irregular Verbs* (with Dan Franklin and Terry Yokota). Dr. Lester is Eastern Washington University professor emeritus of English and former chair. He obtained his B.A. in philosophy and English literature at Pomona College and his Ph.D. in English linguistics from U.C. Berkeley. He also holds an M.B.A. from the University of Hawaii.